—The Decorative Designs of —

C.F.A.VOYSEY

Voysey in his study at The Orchard, Chorley Wood, Hertfordshire, c.1900.

—The Decorative Designs of—
C. F. A. VOYSEY

From The Drawings Collection,
The British Architectural Library,
The Royal Institute of British Architects.

Stuart Durant

NEW YORK

For Ruth, Miriam, Owen and Galia

First published in the United States of America in 1991 by
RIZZOLI INTERNATIONAL PUBLICATIONS, INC.
300 Park Avenue South, New York, NY 10019

Copyright © The Lutterworth Press, 1990
All color illustrations © RIBA
Text © Stuart Durant 1990

First published in Great Britain 1990 by
The Lutterworth Press

Library of Congress Cataloging-in-Publication Data

Durant, Stuart.
    The decorative designs of C.F.A. Voysey / Stuart Durant.
        p.   cm.
    Includes bibliographical references.
    ISBN 0-8478-1301-0
    1. Voysey, Charles F.A., 1857-1941 - Themes, motives. 2. Design -
England - History - 19th century. 3. Design - England - History - 20th
century. I. Title.
NK 1535. N68D8 1991
745.4' 492 - dc20
                                                        90-40304
                                                            CIP

Printed and bound in Hong Kong

—Contents—

Introduction —— 6

Chronological Outline —— 8

Biography —— 9

List of Surviving Buildings —— 29

Manufacturers and Retailers —— 29

Bibliography —— 30

Colour Plates —— 33

—Introduction—

Voysey excelled at decorative design. During the closing years of the last century, and the early ones of the present - when he was among the busiest of architects - Voysey sold many decorative designs to leading manufacturers. After the end of the First World War, when he could find no clients for his buildings, Voysey continued to produce decorative designs. Desperately poor, he tried to sell these to maintain a modest standard of living.

The Drawings Collection of the Royal Institute of British Architects has a remarkable collection of drawings by C.F.A. Voysey in its impressive holdings. It is the most complete record of the work of any architect from the period of the Arts and Crafts ascendancy. There are 931 entries in Joanna Symonds's invaluable 1975 catalogue of the Voysey drawings. Almost a quarter of these relate to designs for wallpapers, carpets or textiles.

Only a few architects - like Charles Rennie Mackintosh, Henry van de Velde, Josef Hoffmann or Hector Guimard - shared with Voysey the same degree of versatility - the ability to design furniture, metalwork, fabrics, wallpapers, carpets - the whole - which eluded architects as accomplished as Lutyens. Baillie Scott, perhaps Voysey's principal rival - was also an excellent decorative designer. But unlike Voysey, he appears to have sold few of his designs to manufacturers. It is true that Frank Lloyd Wright was also a versatile designer, with an original decorative sense - but Wright's output as a designer of decoration was limited. The Voysey designs for decoration in the RIBA collection span a period of some forty-three years - the date 1887 is attributed to the earliest design.

There is another collection of Voysey decorative designs. This is in the Print Room of the Victoria and Albert Museum. But this is an 'edited' collection - the selection was made by Voysey. The RIBA decorative designs are those which were found among Voysey's other drawings.

The fact that the designs in the RIBA collection were not necessarily intended by Voysey for posterity makes them of especial interest. What has been rejected for artistic or even commercial reasons is invariably revealing. It is possible that some designs were never really intended for sale. Did Voysey seriously imagine that an early wallpaper covered with fearsome, fire-breathing devils would be saleable to any but the most eccentric of manufacturers? Or another early wallpaper showing angels with their feet and wings being tickled by small devils?

Might these curious designs be psychologically revealing? Such oddities are often accorded special significance by historians. A plausible explanation for such designs is that they were mere exercises in design - intended only to amuse friends or clients. Or perhaps to display virtuosity in transforming unpromising material into decoration. (Ruskin once illustrated an example of how blots and squiggles could be transformed into decoration - in The Two Paths, 1859. Without enthusiasm, it ought to be said.) Besides, it is unlikely that Voysey, the loyal son of a clergyman dismissed for preaching that there was no Hell, would have taken the idea of the Devil at all seriously.

Having said this, a few of Voysey's early designs do nevertheless evoke some slight feelings of unease. Obviously, to attempt precise iconographical readings in such cases would be hazardous. But it is worth bearing in mind that, while the imagery favoured by Arts and Crafts designers was almost invariably pastoral and reassuringly benign, there was a darker side even to the mind of the central figure of the movement - William Morris. This is certainly manifested in some of his fanciful tales, if not in his designs. The same might be said of the work of a painter who was intimately bound up with Morris and the Arts and Crafts - Edward Burne Jones. One could well speak of their unconscious, as well as conscious, evocations of evil, or despair. Ruskin - whose ideas permeated the thinking of all concerned with the Arts and Crafts - was perturbed by thoughts that his age was inherently evil and that cosmic retribution was near at hand. This is exemplified in 'The Storm Clouds of the Nineteenth Century' - his two disturbing, even prophetic, lectures delivered at the Royal Institution in 1884. Oscar Wilde and Robert Louis Stevenson also attempted to represent, by symbol and allegory, the sicknesses of their society. Voysey, who had a high degree of sensibility, would have been aware of the unhappiness and alienation of his times. Friends, like A.H. Mackmurdo, in the Century Guild - with which he was closely associated at the beginning of his career in the early 1880s - certainly were.

Voysey's attitudes were affected by the cultural climate of his youth. His father's unorthodox religion seems to have stood somewhere between a muted Anglicanism and fully fledged scientific humanism. Such compromises are inevitable in times of change. Voysey grew up when scientific materialism was advancing inexorably - his love of pastoral imagery can be seen as typical of the late-nineteenth-century retreat from materialism.

Acknowledgements.
From the Drawings Collection of the Royal Institute of British Architects I should like to thank: Jill Lever, Curator; Dr. Neil Bingham, Deputy Curator; Jane Preger, Exhibitions Officer; Andrew Norris, Drawings Assistant. I should also like to thank: Dr. Jill Allibone, for allowing me to see the manuscript of her study of George Devey; Pat Craddock; James Bettley; David Game; Lilah and Peter Clarke; and Margaret Slythe, Head of Library, Dulwich College. My especial thanks are due to John Brandon-Jones, architect, the authority on Voysey, for reading my manuscript and making helpful comments. *Frontispiece* by kind permission of the Librarian of the British Architectural Library/RIBA. All other photographs were taken by Jeremy Butler.

Chronological Outline
of Voysey's Life

1857 28 May, born at Hessle, near Hull, the son of Rev Charles Voysey, 1828-1912 and Frances (Edlin).

1864 Rev C. Voysey appointed Vicar of Healaugh, near York. Publishes unorthodox sermon.

1869-71 Rev C. Voysey deprived of his living by the Chancellor's Court of the Diocese of York because of his unorthodox preaching. Sentence upheld by Judicial Committee of Privy Council. He refuses to retract, and the family move to London, where he starts preaching at St George's Hall, Langham Place

1872 C.F.A. Voysey enters Dulwich College as a day boy. Withdrawn after 18 months and taught thereafter by a private tutor

1874 11 May, Voysey articled to John Pollard Seddon (1827-1906), an architect with a successful mainly ecclesiastical practice

1877 Begins taking minor commissions of his own

1879 Assistant to Henry Saxon Snell (1830-1904), specialist in the design of institutions

1880-81 Improver (unpaid assistant) to George Devey, the country house architect

1881 (or early 1882) sets up his own practice in Westminster

1882-84 Worked on project for sanatorium in Teignmouth (illustrated in *Dekorative Kunst*, I, 1897, 249)

1883 Under the influence of A.H. Mackmurdo (1851-1942) began producing decorative designs (earliest design sold to Jeffrey & Co, leading wallpaper manufacturer)

1885 Married Mary Maria Evans. First home in Blandford Rd, Bedford Park. Later moved to Streatham Hill. Designs for his cottage-studio probably date from this year (*The Studio*, IV, 1894, 34)

1890-91 Moved to Melina Place, St John's Wood

1891 Designs house for J.W. Forster in Bedford Park

1891-92 Designs pair of houses in Hans Rd, Knightsbridge, his only town houses

1893 Designs covers for *The Studio* - which is to publicise Voysey's work for over a decade. Designs Perrycroft, Colwall, Malvern, for J.W. Wilson, MP. This costs £4,900, his first large commission

1895 Designs Annesley Lodge, Platt's Lane, Hampstead, for his father

1896 Designs large house (known variously as Merlshanger, Wancote and Grey Friars) for Julian Sturgis, the writer, on the Hog's Back near Guildford. Numerous illustrations of this house were to be published

1897 Extensive and profusely illustrated article published on Voysey in *Dekorative Kunst* (Munich). Designs New Place, Haslemere, for A.M. Stedman

1898 Designs Broadleys (used in the film of *The French Lieutenant's Woman* as a symbol of 19th-century enlightenment) Lake Windermere, for A. Currer Briggs

1899 Designs Spade House, Sandgate for H.G. Wells, and The Orchard, Chorley Wood, Hertfordshire, for himself and his family

1902 Designs factory for Sandersons, wallpaper manufacturers, at Chiswick. This is his largest building

1903-14 Designs a number of houses, enters competition for Government Buildings in Ottawa (1913)

1914 Outbreak of First World War. This marks the virtual end of Voysey's architectural practice

1915 *Individuality* published

1918 Writes to Alistair Morton of his 'terrible plight' financially

1923-36 Designs textiles and furniture as well as alterations to his buildings

1924 Elected Master of the Art Workers' Guild

1929 Writes to Morton that he had sold £50 of designs in the previous year. 'The Council of the RIBA have elected me a full fellow - a compliment which will not save me from starving'

1931 Exhibition of work at the Batsford Gallery under the auspices of the *Architectural Review*. The revival of interest in Voysey appears to have begun at about this time

1936 Awarded the distinction of Designer for Industry by the Royal Society for the Arts

1940 Awarded the Royal Gold Medal of the Royal Institute of British Architects

1941 12 February, dies in Winchester

C. F. A. Voysey Archt

Charles Francis Annesley Voysey, 1857-1941, was, perhaps, the best known British architect at the beginning of the twentieth century. He was also renowned as a designer of fabrics, wallpapers and carpets. The Voysey House, with its characteristic decoration and furniture was known throughout Europe and America. It represented, in an architectural form, the new intellectual and artistic enlightenment.

H.G. Wells lived in a Voysey house - Spade House, at Sandgate, near Folkestone, Kent, built in 1899. *The Studio*, a new kind of popular art magazine, with an international outlook as well as an international circulation, helped to make Voysey famous.

While the Voysey style - architectural as well as decorative - is instantly recognizable, it is important to acknowledge that Voysey was part of a movement - the Arts and Crafts. Its influence upon domestic architecture, may be gauged by citing some of the prinicipal names. From the generation that preceded Voysey's - the proto-Arts and Crafts generation - there were George Devey, in whose office Voysey was to work, W. Eden Nesfield and Richard Norman Shaw. Philip Webb, from the same generation, is properly claimed as a true Arts and Crafts architect. From Voysey's own generation one must include: C.R. Ashbee, Cecil Brewer, Ernest Gimson, W.R. Lethaby, Edwin Lutyens, Charles Rennie Mackintosh, Ernest Newton, Barry Parker, E.S. Prior, M.H. Baillie Scott, George Walton and Edgar Wood. So powerful was the impact of the Arts and Crafts movement upon domestic architecture that another thirty, or even forty, important names could be added to the list.

Voysey's fame, unlike that of many of his contemporaries, never entirely faded away - even during the lean years of the Modern Movement. In 1931, John Betjeman wrote about him with enthusiasm in *The Architectural Review*. In 1934, the architect Raymond McGrath, a champion of the new movement, praised him highly in the historical part of his *Twentieth Century Houses* which, apart from Frederick Etchell's 1927 translation of Le Corbusier's *Vers une Architecture*, of 1923, was the first modernist text accessible to the layperson in Britain. Nikolaus Pevsner in *Pioneers of the Modern Movement* (later to appear as *Pioneers of Modern Design*), which was first published in 1936, recognized Voysey and his achievements - albeit as a precursor of the Modern Movement.

What are the affinities between designing decoration, or pattern, or ornament - call it what one chooses - and designing buildings? The fact is, if one looks outside our present century, or even at the early years of this century, it is easy enough to find architects who were among the best decorative designers of their era. Think of Palladio, Inigo Jones, Nash, Soane.... Or, in the nineteenth century, Pugin, William Butterfield, William Burges, E.W. Godwin, Louis Sullivan, Hector Guimard, the young Henry Van de Velde.... Yet the skills now considered necessary for designing pattern, or architecture, are assumed to be widely different. Even the most superficial analysis, however, will establish that there is a good deal in common between the processes of organizing a pattern and organizing a building. Architects and decorative designers both need a thorough knowledge of practical geometry, as well as the rules of bilateral and multi-lateral symmetry, and need to know how to organize discrete elements within given spaces. Much architectural design, like pattern design, has always been concerned with two-dimensional organization. Composing a façade, or applying the rules of proportion, have always been taught as if they were two-dimensional activities. Architects and designers both need to understand how the permutation of the components of a design can produce variety. Permutation is an essential part of the designing process.

The question of historic style is far less relevant in the case of Voysey's decoration than it is in the cases of other late nineteenth and early twentieth century designers - particularly run-of-the-mill commercial designers. Designers were then expected to have a complete command of the approved historical and national styles. A sophisticated, though sometimes arid, eclecticism was the outcome. Voysey, however, like other Arts and Crafts designers - Morris, or Webb, or Lethaby - sought to rise above mere style and produce work which, though related to tradition, was autonomous.

The recurring subjects in Voysey's decoration are those of his era. They consist, for the most part, of familiar plants, trees, birds and occasionally animals - very like William Morris's decorative subjects. They function as symbols of a beneficent and abundant nature. Nature was viewed as a reassuring constant during a time of considerable social, political and psychological flux. Voysey's decoration - and decoration has all too often been treated as a minor art form incapable of purveying meaning - is in reality full of meaning. But the language he speaks is of his own age. Voysey is best understood if he is set against the backdrop of his own times.

The Reverend Charles Voysey, 1828-1912

Voysey's father was caught up in the turmoil of his age. Voysey's own responses were often conditioned by the experiences of his father. Voysey was always very close to his father who was a determined and original man. Charles Voysey was the son of an architect - Annesley Voysey, 1794-1834. He was descended from John Wesley's sister - the family tradition of dissent may well

help to explain his subsequent doctrinal quarrel with the church. In 1851, Charles Voysey graduated from St Edmund's Hall, Oxford, and was ordained in the Church of England. In 1852 he married Frances Maria Edlin, the daughter of a banker. There were to be four sons and six daughters. After seven years as curate in Hessle, a suburb of Kingston-upon-Hull - where Voysey was born - he was appointed incumbent to a parish in Jamaica. Annesley Voysey had, in fact, practised in Jamaica and one may assume some long-standing connection. However, he returned to England after a comparatively short time and was appointed to a curacy at Great Yarmouth. We find him in 1864, several curacies later, mainly in poor parishes, appointed vicar of Healaugh, which is some six miles from the cathedral city of York.

In 1861, while curate at St Mark's, Whitechapel, Charles Voysey preached against the doctrine of eternal punishment. But in 1864, soon after his arrival at Healaugh, he published a sermon - 'Is every statement in the Bible about our Heavenly Father true?' As a result of such unorthodox preaching, which amounted almost to heresy in the minds of the church authorities, he was ultimately summoned, in 1869, to present himself before the Chancellor's Court of the Diocese of York. He was deprived of his living. Voysey subsequently put his case against this decision to the Privy Council, which again passed judgement against him on February 11, 1871. He was given a week in which to retract his errors. He would not. Furthermore, costs were awarded against him.

Even before the judgement came into effect, Charles Voysey had begun to hold services in St George's Hall, Langham Place. He quickly attracted followers and a 'Voysey Establishment Fund' was organized.

Voysey was a courageous man. He could have lived out his life as a country clergyman, with a secure living - certainly with enough money to bring up his family in a congenial middle-class manner. He could also have hoped to advance within the hierarchy of the church. For there is no doubt that his talents had at one time been recognized by his superiors. Charles Voysey chose instead a difficult and potentially isolated path. He suffered for his beliefs. His family, including young Voysey, must have suffered with him.

The Voysey affair was one of the church scandals of the day, although certainly not the equal in its impact of the Gorham Judgement, or of Charles Kingsley's unpleasant libel of John Henry Newman. The story of the Voysey affair would be worth recounting even if it merely shed light upon the childhood circumstances of Voysey. The nature of Charles Voysey's teaching was, however, in itself remarkable. Because, in addition, it influenced Voysey's subsequent attitudes, it is worthy of more than cursory examination.

The startling fact is that Charles Voysey, far from developing an unorthodox variety of Anglican theology, founded what amounted to a new religion. By 1885 he had collected a not inconsiderable following and had acquired his own church - to be known as The Theistic Church, Swallow Street, which is a small street linking Piccadilly with Regent Street. A far from unfashionable venue, one might think. Charles Voysey published his ideas vociferously. His collected sermons - in ten volumes - were readily available and his defence of his position at York was in print thirty years after the event. Charles Voysey's teaching, however, is most accessible in *Theism: or the Religion of Common Sense*, 1894, which had first appeared as a series of weekly articles in *The Weekly Times and Echo*.

Theism was 'not only a theology, but a religion'. Theists, unlike many churchmen, positively welcomed the discoveries of science. The theory of evolution, even its doctrine of the survival of the fittest, could be embraced. Theism itself, Charles Voysey claimed, was the product of the evolutionary advance of modern religious thought. Traditional revelation was suspect and to be discarded.

The God of the Theists was all goodness. The pains and sorrows of this world were simply the means by which God 'has raised and is raising us from a merely animal or savage state'. While Charles Voysey accepted that there was an after-life, he discouraged speculation upon its nature. Above all, his God was neither angry, nor vengeful. Mediators, priests and Christ himself, were unnecessary between man and God. 'An incarnation like that of Jesus Christ . . . would create a gulf between God and men which never existed . . . if God be our Father in deed and truth, mediation and intercession would only distress and insult Him'. He cited the view that the 'deification of Jesus is the grand historical testimony to the meanness of man's thoughts about God'.

Charles Voysey's Theism accorded with the mood of 'sweetness and light' which is associated with the thinking of the cultivated middle classes of the 1870s and 1880s. Theism may be seen as emanating as much from the undermining of conventional faith - by the reverberating findings of science - as from biblical criticism. Its essential optimism contrasts strikingly with the pessimism which scientific discovery induced in Ruskin, who pondered upon a statement by Dunning that man, because he possessed carnivorous teeth, was a predator by nature, Ruskin wrote in his diary, on March 29, 1874: 'To such a man, and to the nation believing him, all history is dead - all Art and all Nature . . . . To have the soul of a thief so fastened to one's body . . . '. Charles Voysey retained his equilibrium in the face of Darwinism. Theism was not opposed to 'a single fact' of science.

Let him make a final claim for Theism: 'Theism, like all other forms of belief is anthropomorphic, and must in the nature of things be so. That is why it is not final, but must one day grow into something higher and better. But this is why it is better than the Christian faith . . . its conception of God is unspeakably higher and more true than those distinctive conceptions of God which are essentially "Christian".' With the death of Charles Voysey on July 20, 1912, Dr Walter Walsh led the Theist congregation. But soon there was schism. The Swallow Street church was closed in 1913 and the building soon demolished.

Voysey was twelve when the drama at Healaugh began to unfold. It must have permanently scarred him. It also tempered and hardened him.

Voysey's early education

Voysey was first tutored by his father - a common enough practice in clerical families. Charles Voysey was, in fact, an experienced teacher and had run a school at Hessle with his brother. However, after the loss of the living at Healaugh, when the Voysey family moved to London, Voysey was sent as a day-boy to Dulwich College which was, by all accounts, an enlightened institution.

There had been a good deal of ambitious building at the school shortly before Voysey's arrival there. Charles Barry, junior, 1823-1900, the son of Sir Charles Barry, was the architect. Work had begun in 1866 and had been completed when Voysey joined Dulwich in 1872. The style was North Italian Renaissance and rich in terracotta detail. Barry's Dulwich College is not without affinities with Captain Fowkes' contributions to the South Kensington Museum - now the Victoria and Albert Museum - which was conceived at much the same time. Whatever young Voysey thought of Barry's work, there is no denying that he was exposed - at an impressionable age - to an exciting, if rather 'intemperate' building, as one critic observed.

J.C.L. Sparkes was Art Master at Dulwich. He appears to have been an inspiring teacher. Stanhope Forbes, 1857-1947, the founder of the Newlyn School of *plein air* painting - painter of 'The Health of the Bride', 1889, a delightful genre picture, as popular now as the day it was first exhibited, was a fellow pupil of Sparkes. Another was Henry La Thangue, 1859-1929 - best known for his picture 'The Man with the Scythe', 1895, in which an old countryman with a scythe passes the gate of a cottage garden, where a child, seemingly dying of consumption, sits propped in a chair. The intimation of approaching death is clear. La Thangue was said to have combined successfully 'French techniques and British sentiment'. The diminished reputations of Stanhope Forbes and La Thangue are now reviving. In their own day, however, they were among the most esteemed of post Pre-Raphaelite young painters.

Sparkes, so able to recognize potential in the young, evidently did not suggest a career in art for Voysey. His figure drawing - though he could only have drawn from plaster casts at Dulwich - though passable, would not have impressed even the percipient Sparkes. Voysey was never destined to be a painter. Might Sparkes have suggested architecture to Voysey's family as a future career for their son?

Sparkes, in ensuring that art was taken seriously at Dulwich, must be accounted as an early representative of the nineteenth century enlightenment. For, despite the influence of Ruskin, art was not generally a highly-rated activity in boys' schools.

Even with what one must assume to have been the benign presence of Sparkes, Voysey was withdrawn from Dulwich and placed with a private tutor. He was evidently not suited to competitive academic life. According to Martin S. Briggs, in 'Voysey and Blomfield, a study in contrasts', (*The Builder*, volume 176, January 14, 1949), Voysey did not learn to read until he was fourteen. Certainly, his spelling was sometimes curious. Possibly he was dyslexic - although retrospective diagnosis of a condition, especially one which not all psychologists actually recognize, is dangerous. It is also possible that Voysey's apparent academic under-achievement stemmed from the unsettling effects of the Healaugh case.

At all events, architecture was selected as an appropriate career. There were no qualifying examinations in the 1870s. The study of architecture was not considered likely to bring about academic stress. Voysey himself said, according to John Brandon-Jones, that the fact architecture was chosen for him, was simply because his grandfather, Annesley Voysey had been an architect.

Architectural Education in the 1870s

In the 1870s there was no formal system of architectural education in Britain. Aspiring architects were apprenticed, or articled. There was no equivalent of the Parisian Ecole des Beaux Arts, with its complicated and graduated exercises in composition and styles. Nor was there a British institution - like the Beaux Arts - that planned to formulate a rational architecture expressing the mores of the nineteenth century.

Articles, or apprenticeships, cost money. Fairly considerable sums, for the time, had to be paid. No doubt there were abuses. Pugin poked fun at the situation in *Contrasts*, 1836. Here he illustrated an architectural emporium in the style of Soane - a 'Temple of Taste and Architectural Repository' - the very epitome of banality. Over a door to the shop is a placard inscribed 'An architect has a vacancy in his office for one pupil - talent of no consequence. Premium £100'.

There was a distinction between those architects who were skilled technicians and those who thought of themselves as members of a burgeoning learned profession. Many architects dealt with the gentry, knew the ways of the gentry, but could not consider themselves gentry. They had an uncertain status like surgeons or apothecaries - socially equivocal professions which fascinated writers like Mrs. Gaskell or Wilkie Collins.

It is instructive to consider the social origins of Voysey's two principal mentors. John Pollard Seddon's father was a successful London cabinet maker; George Devey's was a London solicitor. To turn to the origins of some of the often leading architects of Voysey's youth: William Butterfield's father was a chemist with a shop off the Strand; Owen Jones's father was a prosperous farrier with a scholarly interest in ancient Welsh literature; William Burges' father was a successful marine engineer; and Philip Webb's father was an Oxford surgeon. George Gilbert Scott, like Voysey, came from a clerical background. While Owen Jones was articled to Lewis Vuilliamy and Burges to Edmund Blore - both fashionable and successful - the others were taught by modest enough practitioners.

By the middle of the nineteenth century, part of the necessary education of the ambitious young architect was the undertaking of a lengthy sketching tour of Europe. Voysey, always insular in his outlook, never embarked upon such a tour. Richard Norman Shaw and W. Eden Nesfield actually made early reputations by publishing facsimiles of their continental drawings.

One can merely speculate on what architectural literature Voysey would have read. He evidently read some Ruskin as he mentions him in some of his writings. Did he only read the obligatory *Seven Lamps of Architecture*, 1849? Or *The Stones of Venice*, 1852-3 - with its transcendental and unforgettable chapter 'On the Nature of Gothic'? Voysey spoke of Pugin with respect too. Did he read the stirring polemic of *Contrasts* and laugh at Pugin's amusing caricatures of tedious classicism and mindless eclecticism? There is ample visual evidence that he was acquainted with Pugin's *Glossary of Ecclesiastical Ornament*, first published in 1844, and still a standard work in the 1870s. There is always a little of Pugin's directness and vigour in Voysey's decoration. It is almost inconceivable that there would have not been a copy in Seddon's office. No self-respecting Gothic Revival ecclesiastical architect, whatever he thought of Pugin's buildings, or his beliefs, could be without the *Glossary* - a luscious, even gaudy, compendium which demonstrated the potentialities of symbolic decoration. Voysey would have also probably known Pugin's *Floriated Ornament*, 1849, reprinted in 1875, which showed how botanical illustrations could be transformed into decoration.

John Pollard Seddon, 1827-1906

J.P. Seddon was forty-six when Voysey joined his practice as an articled pupil on May 11, 1874. Voysey was within days of seventeen. He liked Voysey, and Voysey liked him. It could be said that Seddon, with his largely orthodox Anglican ecclesiastical clientele, manifested a commendable degree of liberality in taking on the eldest son of a clergyman who had been dismissed from the church for obstinate disobedience. But much of Seddon's work, particularly when he was a partner with John Pritchard, was in Wales - where dissent, if not outright heresy, was not uncommon. He would certainly have been familiar with, and hence less worried by, unorthodox theological stances than many ecclesiastical architects. Voysey would have been set to work tracing, copying, measuring, observing - 'learning by doing'. In 1874 Seddon was designing country churches in Herefordshire and

Hertfordshire and rebuilding a church in Herefordshire and altering another in Norfolk. He exhibited designs for an orphanage and the interior of a chapel at the Royal Academy in the same year.

Seddon's work was always sober, decent. His buildings are excellent exemplars of sensible mediaevalism applied to nineteenth century circumstances. He is never perverse, like Butterfield, or playful, like Burges. Undoubtedly, his best known building is University College, Aberystwyth, Dyfed - now the University College of Wales. It had been begun initially as The Castle House Hotel in 1864. It is a solemn, not unlikeable, building, with rather simple and original mullions - no doubt designed for reasons of economy. Voysey is said to have designed some decorative panels in cement for the entrance to the South Wing. The building suggests that Seddon would have been well-able to handle other large commissions, had they come his way. His competition designs of 1884 for the Law Courts were not successful, however - the competition was won by George Edmund Street.

Seddon designed many pieces of furniture. As the son of a cabinet-maker, the interest is hardly surprising. He exhibited an elaborate inlaid roll-top desk on the stand of the newly-founded firm of Morris, Faulkner, Marshall and Company at the International Exhibition at South Kensington in 1862. Seddon also designed a cabinet, made by the Morris firm, named 'King René's Honeymoon', which incorporated painted panels by Ford Madox Brown, Burne Jones and Rossetti. Seddon, then, came briefly under the influence of Pre-Raphaelitism. His furniture designs also suggest that he knew Pugin's furniture-from his *Gothic Furniture*, 1835 - his first book, incidentally.

Voysey's furniture bears the imprint of his years with Seddon. His bold use of decorative hinges reminds one of Seddon. So, too, does his fondness for plain panels which rely upon the grain of the wood for their decorative effect. What was, very likely, Voysey's last executed design - an oak dressing table for his niece, the wife of the actor Robert Donat - has a mirror surround shaped like a thirteenth-century trefoil window. It is thoroughly Gothic, or more properly Gothic Revival, in spirit. The dressing table was made in 1934, when Voysey was seventy-seven and when British Modernists were flexing their muscles. Yet he still drew succour from the era which had nurtured him.

Seddon was a competent decorative designer. He designed many encaustic floor tiles for the leading manufacturers of the day. Seddon also designed ecclesiastical embroideries. It is thus certain, quite certain, that Voysey learned the fundamentals of decoration - and Gothic decoration at that - while in the Seddon office. A drawing by Voysey of Seddon's designs for stoneware capitals and bases, for the Fulham Pottery, is to be seen in the Print Room of the Victoria and Albert Museum. The style is Ruskinian and resembles some of the details illustrated in *The Stones of Venice*.

1. John Pollard Seddon.
Design for an encaustic tile panel, for Maw and Co, Broseley, Shropshire.
The Building News, August 22, 1873.

Voysey learned a great deal from Seddon. Not least, he adopted in his architectural thinking, the high moral tone of the committed Puginian, or Ruskinian, Goth. He assisted Seddon for a short while after completing his articles in 1878, but he left the practice fairly soon. Seddon had little in hand for 1879 - a church restoration in Buckinghamshire, the rebuilding of a church in Wales and additions to a cottage. It is possible that the prevailing economic recession was beginning to affect even a predominantly ecclesiastical practice.

Henry Saxon Snell, 1830-1904

After leaving Seddon, Voysey joined the office of Saxon Snell who specialized in the design of hospitals and charitable institutions. The contrast with the Seddon office could not have been more marked, for Snell was essentially a technician - though an able one. He had none of Seddon's artistic leanings and had for a time been an assistant to Joseph Paxton - a fact which would have branded him a member of what Ruskin disparagingly called 'the Steam Whistle Party'. Temperamentally, Voysey was not suited to the Snell office.

Snell's best known building is The Royal Patriotic Boys Orphanage, Wandsworth, 1872 - since 1881 Emmanuel School. It is a solemn, workaday, building, with some Gothic detail and patterned brickwork. The Snell practice was a successful and durable one and under the name of Saxon Snell and Barnard it was to be responsible for the St. Helier Hospital, near Morden, of 1938.

The 1870s had seen the beginning of a great increase in the building of hospitals and schools. As early as 1863, Butterfield, who by then had a considerable reputation, had designed the County Hospital at Winchester. The design of institutional buildings was to become increasingly sophisticated. Saxon Snell himself was the author of two important studies - *Charitable and Parochial Buildings*, 1881, and, with Dr. F.J. Mouat, *Hospital Construction and Management*, 1883.

But Voysey found the work in the Snell office dull. He left after a comparatively short time. Interestingly, one of Voysey's first essays in design, after he had set up on his own, was for a sanatorium in Teignmouth, Devon, which he worked on between 1882 and 1884. No doubt, the technical expertise needed for such a specialized building must have been acquired during the time spent with Snell. The sanatorium project - a patterned brick, stone mullioned, partly half-timbered, building - came to nothing.

George Devey, 1820-1886

Voysey joined the office of George Devey, the designer of country houses, in 1880. Voysey was to spend less than two years in Devey's office, at 123 Bond Street. It was a small office by our standards - there were ten employees. He was an 'improver' - an improver was a young man who, having completed articles, worked to improve his position within the profession. An improver would work for little or, quite frequently, for no payment, in the office of a successful practitioner. Devey was certainly successful. He has, until recently, been somewhat underrated by historians, although Mark Girouard in *The Victorian Country House*, 1971, treats him very respectfully. Jill Allibone's monograph on Devey will put matters right. Devey was unquestionably a major figure. But, like Philip Webb, he was inclined to avoid publicity. Voysey was fortunate indeed to have had the opportunity to observe Devey at work at close quarters.

Devey's clients were generally members of the landed gentry, or the aristocracy. There was also the occasional *nouveau riche* client. Numbered among Devey's clients, at about the time Voysey was in his office, were: Lord Lytton, the Marquis of Lorne, Lord Granville, the Rothschilds, the Duke of Westminster and Mrs. Henrietta Montefiore. Devey had built some eleven fine houses during the decade which had begun in 1870.

Devey was a member of Charles Voysey's Theistic Church. He contributed regularly to church funds, and actually bequeathed £2,000 to the Trustees of the Theistic Church, together with the same amount to Charles Voysey himself. These were large sums in the 1880s. It was surely because of Devey's connection with Theism that Voysey was able to arrange to work in the Devey office. A spell in an important office is always a good way in which to begin a career. Voysey was twenty-two and impressionable and eager.

By 1880, when Voysey joined Devey's office, the Gothic tide had receded. Gothic had become unfashionable for country houses, as well as for secular buildings in general. The mediaevalising country house style of Pugin, Gilbert Scott, Butterfield, Teulon, James Brooks, or Burges, was decidedly *passé*. Norman Shaw, Nesfield and Devey were the country house architects of the day. Their designs subtly alluded to the past, rather than attempting to recreate it, in the scenographic manner of their predecesors. The fashionable style in the 1870s and 1880s, was picturesque and eclectic. Shaw's Cragside, Northumberland, of 1870-1884, for the armament manufacturer William Armstrong, is as determinedly picturesque as mad Ludwig's Bavarian hill-top castle. Cragside serves as a splendid, if extreme, exemplar of picturesque eclecticism.

Independently of Shaw and Nesfield, Devey appears to have arrived at an architectural style which is quite close to their versions of what was popularly called 'Queen Anne'. His Denne Hill, near Canterbury, Kent, of 1871-75, incorporates the kind of elaborately shaped red brick gables found in Kew Palace, the Royal Botanic Gardens, Kew, in actuality an early seventeenth century London merchant's house, which were so beloved of Shaw.

As well as being *au courant* with modish, eclectic, Queen Anne - 'the style favoured by aesthetes', according to Walter Hammond, writing in 1881 - Devey was also an innovator. In 1876 he designed a series of five variant house types for the Spencer Estate, for an abortive middle-class housing scheme in Northampton - a kind of projected East Midlands Bedford Park. Devey's

semi-detached and terrace houses are particularly interesting. They are less affected, in terms of style, than Shaw's contemporary work in Bedford Park - the prototypical garden suburb. Devey's Northampton houses seem to be authentic precursors of the turn-of-the-century Letchworth Garden City houses of Barry Parker and Raymond Unwin, or their later houses for Hampstead Garden Suburb - or for that matter, Baillie Scott's, or Geoffrey Lucas's. Like them, Devey was accomplished in adapting vernacular features for modern use. The Drawings Collection possesses many sketches of vernacular architecture by Devey.

Voysey's first essays in domestic design - his design for example, for a medium-sized country house, with diapered brickwork and a stone base, illustrated in *The British Architect*, XXXI, 1889, has more than a passing resemblance to a Devey house. So, too, does his design for a half-timbered house for himself of around 1885, which was never built. (See figures 2 and 5.)

Devey evidently thought highly of Voysey. After about a year in his office, Devey had enough confidence in him to entrust him with a commission. It was a small one - a pair of cheap cottages in Northamptonshire, on land which Devey had bought. Voysey was made responsible for contracting builders, paying wages and supervising construction. Were these cottages identifiable - if they still exist - they would shed light on Voysey's development at a most interesting and critical stage.

2. Design for a house with an octagonal hall, before 1889. *Dekorative Kunst*, V, 1897 (reproduced from *The British Architect*, XXXI, 1889.)
This house, which was never built, was designed when Voysey was still under Devey's influence.

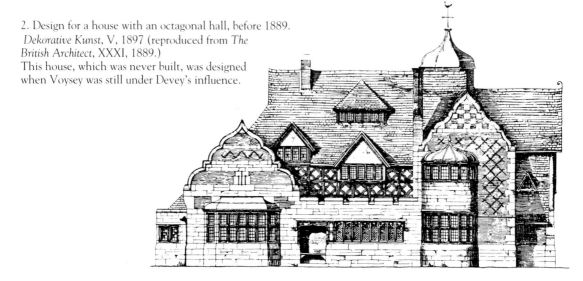

Devey's patrons were quite unlike the progressive but, less well-heeled, late Victorians who were to become Voysey's own clients. Nevertheless, Voysey would have learned from Devey how an architect should deal with sophisticated and demanding people. The manner, in fact, in which Voysey conducted his practice was to remain Victorian in its character.

Voysey's own practice

In 1882, Voysey set up his own architectural practice. His first office was at Queen Anne's Gate. Soon, however, he was to move. His removal card is instructive. Voysey declares that he 'hath now removed unto ye more commodious premises situate at ye Broadway Chambers Westminster'. Here, 'from henceforth all ye craft of ye master architect will be exercised'. Such affectation may be forgiven as a youthful excess. He entered a competition for the Admiralty offices in Whitehall, but, hardly surprisingly, his design was unplaced. His design for the Teignmouth Sanatorium, as we have already seen, came to nothing. He published an etched portrait of his father. . . . Proper commissions, of course, do not always come easily to young architects at the beginnings of their careers. Voysey must, however, have had surveys and alterations to partly occupy him. Even when working for Seddon he had been undertaking these on his own account.

It was during this fallow period, that Voysey turned to decorative design. But before embarking upon an account of Voysey the decorative designer, his emergence as an architect needs to be considered. His attitudes towards decorative design are, besides, closely allied to his attitudes towards architecture. He was a whole person - there is, in truth, no disparity between his highly personal architectural style and his decoration.

Voysey, as an architect, was an entirely new kind of phenomenon. He was certainly the earliest popular architect - popular, that is, among his own contemporaries. Like his father, Voysey had considerable skill as a self-publicist. He had demonstrated it even with that curious removal card. Voysey took every opportunity to present himself to the widest possible public. This is not to say that he was an extrovert - in the way that Pugin, or Le Corbusier, were. But Voysey, survivor that he was, knew how to exploit every conceivable channel to make his work known.

Voysey and 'The Studio'

In the 1880s and 1890s there were a number of specialist magazines for architects - *The British Architect*, *The Builder*, *The Building News*. . . . Then there were the art magazines *The Art-Journal*, which was long-established, and, by the time Voysey was beginning to emerge, a trifle stuffy. There were also *The Magazine of Art*, *The Portfolio*, *The Journal of Decorative Art* and *Decoration* - which, under the editorship of J. Moyr Smith seemed to almost caricature the mannerisms of the Aesthetic Movement. But *The Studio* was to become the principal vehicle through which the Voysey style became known to a very large international public.

The Studio, which first appeared in April 1893, was an altogether new kind of art magazine. Like *The Strand Magazine*, first issued in January 1891, which contained 'stories and articles by the best British writers . . . translations from the best foreign authors . . . illustrated by eminent artists', *The Studio* made extensive use of the half tone process for reproducing illustrations. This process, which had become possible on a commercial scale in the late 1880s, meant that the expensive and tedious processes of steel or wood engraving could be dispensed with. In addition, because a photographic process was involved, near-facsimiles of artists', or architects', drawings could now be published - without the all too often subjective, and frequently insensitive, interpretations of engravers. Architects and designers who could draw attractively came into their own. Voysey was a case in point. Since the invention of the half-tone process, the architect's sketch became an accepted art form. Its impact upon architecture has yet to be fully evaluated.

But there was more than a mere technical resemblance between *The Strand Magazine*, and *The Studio*. Both magazines were topical, informative and unpompous. Gleeson White, 1852-1898, himself a designer, edited *The Studio* with extraordinary flair during its early years. Charles Holme, 1848-1923, was the publisher of *The Studio*. He was an entrepreneur - a former wool merchant and importer of bric-à-brac from the East - with an enthusiasm for the arts. In 1889 he had moved into William Morris's famous Red House, which had been designed by Philip Webb in 1859. Both Gleeson White and Holme cultivated Voysey.

The designer Frederick L. Mayers, who was a young man in the 1890s, described the impact of *The Studio*. He was writing in a seemingly unlikely place - *Carpet Designs and Designing*, 1934. Mayers remembers his 'delight when he turned over the pages of that first number'. He found that *The Studio* was 'something more significant than just another magazine for the dilettante, and that "Fine" and "Applied" art were given equal prominence'. It became more apparent with each succeeding number 'how valuable a "go-between" it was between art workers and the public . . . '. The name of 'many an art worker who was scarcely known outside the immediate circle in which he worked became . . . almost a household word'. Mayers noted the impact Aubrey Beardsley's black and white illustrations made: 'Whether it was supremely good judgement, or good luck, which brought Beardsley's work into the first number, it decided the success of the "Studio" and made Beardsley instantly famous . . . '. *The Studio* made Voysey famous too.

The Studio appealed to the rising generation of the artistically literate. Young people, one conjectures, whose parents had read Ruskin in the sixties and seventies and had given their children the illustrated books of Walter Crane, Randolph Caldecott, or Kate Greenaway to look at in their nurseries.

Voysey made an appearance in the first number of *The Studio*, of April 1893, with illustrations of a wallpaper for Jeffrey & Co. and a fretted metal grille for Essex & Company's wallpaper showrooms. He made his first major appearance, however, in the September issue, the sixth, in a lengthy interview conducted, one can assume, by Gleeson White. Voysey spoke about his approach to decorative design. It may well

3. Trade mark for Essex & Company, wallpaper manufacturers, London.
Dekorative Kunst, I, 1897.
Essex & Company were early patrons of Voysey - he designed many wallpapers for the firm. R.W. Essex, the managing director, commissioned him to design his own house which, however, was completed by Walter Cave.

be that this is the earliest verbatim record of an interview with a designer to be published. The idea of the published interview would surely have come from *The Strand*.

Voysey designed the cover of *The Studio*. It shows two figures - one representing Beauty, holding a lily, the other representing Use holding, of all things, the governor which regulated the speed of a steam engine. The figures, Burne Jones-like and asexual, are embracing - indicating that there need be no conflict between function and aesthetic excellence. Voysey's reputation was to grow with that of *The Studio*. Both were soon to have an enormous international reputation. Both, too, were to have their imitators.

The Voysey House

The most important element in bringing about Voysey's success was the Voysey House. *The Studio* played a great part in making it widely known. The first appearance of the Voysey House was in the October issue of the 1894 *Studio*. It was a project for a house for himself and his young wife. It had probably been designed in 1885. The house is half-timbered - 'solid and tarred, bedded in and filled between with breeze concrete'. The roof was of green slate and the external woodwork was bright green - the colour which Voysey was always to favour. The green, it was claimed, would 'harmonize with the greens of surrounding trees and hills'. Mouldings were generally omitted. Ventilation was by way of large ducts at the side of the chimneys - Voysey had learned about ventilation from Snell; it was a speciality of his. The picturesque little house was buttressed. This, essentially, was the Voysey House.

The 1897 issue of *The Studio* contained a ten-page article on Voysey - 'The Revival of English Domestic Architecture: The Work of Mr C.F.A. Voysey'. It is is signed 'G'. Voysey's well-known house in Bedford Park, for J.W. Forster, of 1891, is illustrated - rough-cast and perfectly, but unfamiliarly, proportioned. It is confidently inserted among Norman Shaw's red-brick Queen Anne (see figure 6). There is also a perspective of the L-shaped house that Voysey built for his father in Platt's Lane, Hampstead - might the Devey legacy have paid for it? It is a typical Voysey house - unornamented and informal. It is buttressed in the Voysey manner (see figure 9). 'G' explained Voysey's reasons: 'to save the cost of thicker walls for the lower storey of his buildings . . although . . . Mr Voysey would no more dream of adding a superfluous buttress than he would add an unnecessary panel of cheap ornament.'

'G' emphasised Voysey's ability to build cheaply but well. 'It is no exaggeration to say that some of the entirely delightful houses he has called into being would compare favourably in cost with the miser-

4. Cover design for the first bound volume of *The Studio*, 1893. This design also appears on the cover of the first number, April 1893.

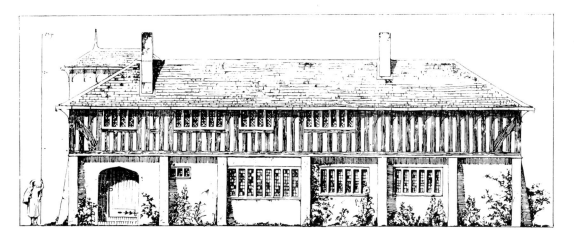

5. Design for Voysey's own cottage, c1885.
Dekorative Kunst, V, 1897.
This was never built. A slightly different version of this, together with plans, was illustrated in *The Studio*, October, 1894.

6. House for J.W. Forster at Bedford Park, 1891
Illustrated in *The Studio*, XI, June 1897
Described originally as an artist's cottage, the house
contrasted vividly with Richard Norman Shaw's
redbrick Queen Anne. A wing added in 1894 has
somewhat diminished the impact.

able shams of the jerry-builder. To beat the
vulgar and badly constructed dwelling - on
economic as well as artistic grounds - is a
notable achievement. But that Mr Voysey
has done it more than once remains an
abiding evidence that art may not only be
obedient to the demands of common sense,
but that it is able to use worthy materials
honestly, and give you a lasting structure as
cheaply as the most scamping rival. . . .'

The first extensive continental account
of Voysey's work was an anonymous article
which appeared in *Dekorative Kunst*. This
was a Munich monthly founded in 1897 and
edited by H. Bruckmann and J.H. Meier-
Graefe - the founder of the magazine *Pan*. It
was closely modelled on *The Studio*. The
article, which appeared in the sixth number
of the magazine, contains copious illustrations of Voysey's architectural projects,
furniture and textiles and wallpapers. The
cost of making the fifty or so half-tone
blocks would have been considerable. The
article was the most ambitious which *Dekorative Kunst* had attempted. Its publication
indicates quite clearly the high esteem in
which Voysey was held in German-speak-

ing Europe. He evidently collaborated very
closely with the writer of the article - might
it have been Hermann Muthesius, the future author of *Das Englische Haus*, who was
in London at the time? Four of Voysey's
important houses are illustrated - Perrycroft
(1893), Broadleys (1898), New Place (1897)
and Norney (1897). Earlier designs are illustrated too, including the house which
had appeared in *The British Architect* in 1889
(see figure 2), his own unbuilt studio cottage (see figure 5), as well as the Teignmouth
sanatorium project. The illustration of these
unexecuted projects, in styles he had partly
abandoned, seems, at first sight, curious.
But Voysey had a feeling for his personal
history.

Horace Townsend, in 'Notes on Country and Suburban Houses designed by C.F.A.
Voysey', in the April issue of *The Studio*,
1899, presented the Voysey House in its
final form. The article is illustrated with
seven examples - there were Broadleys and
Moor Crag, the two important Windermere
houses of 1898, as well as four projects
which were never realized. Voysey often
commissioned professional perspective artists to represent his houses. No doubt these
were intended to impress his clients, but it
seems likely that he also had the ulterior
motive of seeing them published.

The six houses must have made an extraordinary impression - they still do. Ruskin
wrote in *Fors Clavigera*, in 1874, of the need
'to let in the light' and 'to guide and admini-
ster the sunshine'. Voysey, a 'stickler for
light', was letting in the 'sunshine' as no
architect before him. William Morris in
News From Nowhere, 1890, talked of the
impact that the architecture of the twenty-
first century had made in his dream: 'I was
exhilarated to a pitch that I had never yet
reached, I fairly chuckled for pleasure'. The
buildings were 'handsome and generously
solid . . . countryfied . . . like yeomens'
dwellings'. The Voysey House was close to
the buildings in Morris's vision of the future.

Townsend, a regular contributor to *The
Studio*, described Voysey as a 'new architect'. He meant the kind of architect who
designed everything for his houses. He cited
E.W. Godwin, 1833-1886, who had designed

Whistler's White House, as someone who had overturned the absurd theory that the architect who wandered from 'the strait and narrow path and took to designing furniture, wallpapers, and so forth, had committed a species of professional suicide'. Voysey's decorative work was 'epoch making' - an expression, which for once, seems appropriate. Townsend asserted: 'His furniture, with its broad simple effects, its reliance on proportion, its eschewal of useless ornament, and its strikingly original lines, has helped to form a school of its own, while his wallpapers and textiles strike an equally personal and individual note. . . .'

Townsend wrote of Voysey's 'simplicity of thought and perfection of detail'. Then there was his 'deliberate avoidance of style'. With hindsight, it is easy to say that Voysey did not so much avoid style as invent a style - and a distinctive one at that. Let Townsend continue: 'by no slavish adherance to tradition has any living, breathing, architectural style come into being'. Of course, Voysey learned from the past. Nevertheless the sheer newness of the Voysey style, within the confines of its time, still strikes one most forcibly.

The Voysey House became famous internationally. Hermann Muthesius in *Das Englische Haus* 1904-05, which still remains the most useful survey of the English revival in domestic architecture, illustrated some of Voysey's best work. Voysey also appeared in Muthesius's *Das Moderne Landhaus . . .* 1905 (This looks very like a German version of the popular house book, *The British*

7. Design for a fretted metal panel for a staircase, in a house in Hans Road, Knightsbridge, designed by Voysey, for Archibald Grove, 1891-2. Julian Sturgis lived in this house.
The Studio, I, September, 1893.

Home of Today, 1904, edited by W. Shaw Sparrow. Here, of course, Voysey also features prominently.) In *Das Moderne Landhaus* Voysey was the most illustrated British architect - he is followed by Mackintosh, Ernest Newton, Baillie Scott, George Walton and Edgar Wood. It is interesting to see how 'British', in spirit, some of the work of German and Austrian architects actually is. By 1905, the lessons of the British domestic revival had been well absorbed. One senses this in the work of Leopold Bauer, Peter Behrens, Josef Hoffmann, Bernard Pankok, Bruno Paul, Hans Poelzig, Paul Troost and Hans Vollmer; as well as Gesellius, Lindgren and Saarinen, the Helsinki partnership. While Voysey evidently had European admirers, he did not have many actual imitators. However, the Viennese architects, Josef Frank and Robert Oerley, who became prominent just before the outbreak of the First World War, designed houses which are in the Voysey spirit.

8. Perrycroft, Colwall, Malvern, a house for J.W. Wilson, M.P., 1893.
Dekorative Kunst, V, 1897.
The first of Voysey's larger houses.

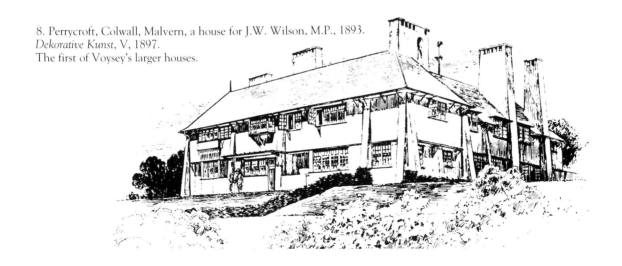

9. Annesley Lodge, Platt's Lane, Hampstead, 1895.
For Voysey's father, the Rev. Charles Voysey.
The Studio, XI, June 1897.
For Voysey buttresses were not an affectation - they enabled him to build lighter walls at ground-floor level, thus saving costs.

Voysey's Writings

With his rise to fame, Voysey felt the need to set out the theoretical - and ethical - basis of his thinking. Writing did not come easily to him. But he thought carefully about what he had to say and his sincerity and idealism are never in doubt.

In 'Ideas in Things', two lectures which are reproduced in *The Arts connected with Building*, 1909, edited by T. Raffles Davison, he railed against materialism. Materialism, which induced an excessive craving for sensation, prompted us to disregard reason. Sometimes his arguments are tenuous - as when he claimed that smooth polished, surfaces were 'materialistic', because they could be produced 'without brains'. In a sense, this is the Arts and Crafts argument, but stated tortuously.

An interesting passage in 'Ideas in Things' seems to savour a little of his father: 'The theory of evolution has disclosed . . . that all organisers are moving in the direction of greater fitness and harmony of condition. It is essential to fitness that objects should minister to our spiritual growth . . . '. This quite clumsy attempt to reconcile the material and spiritual antinomies is characteristic of the era.

On occasions, Voysey could be amusing. Here he is on modern domestic architecture. Most of our houses looked like 'spectres that came and went in the twinkling of an eye, angularity and an infinite variety of shapes and proportions jutting out at you with surprising wildness, as if they were waving their arms impatiently and angrily . . .to add to their complexity they are composed of an infinite number of differently coloured materials and textures . . . . It is our mad rush for wealth and material things that feeds on advertisement, until our very houses shout at us for attention'. In 1909, houses like those Voysey caricatures were appearing in droves in the prosperous suburbs.

Individuality, published in 1915, was Voysey's lengthiest piece of writing. It is nevertheless a small book without illustrations and a comparatively short text. Voysey was fifty-seven and his career had been blighted by the war.

The influences of Charles Voysey's religious teaching can be found on almost every page of *Individuality*. The book is not really a book on design. It is a series of statements of belief with some of the quality of the religious tract about them. Voysey begins with the statement: 'Let us assume there is a beneficent power that is all good and perfectly loving and that our existence here is for growing individual characters.' How like his father, who talked of 'a God intent on the highest welfare of his creation', he sounds. 'Dogma', said Voysey, 'is deadening to progressive thought'. Surely, that was said in response to his boyhood recollections of the tribulations of his father, who had suffered at the hands of dogmatists.

Voysey's hatred of materialism surfaces again: 'A generation or so is devoted to material needs and brings forth the engine and the motor and machines in all their manifold forms, making even man into a machine'. This is Ruskinian. A new form of spirituality would surely arise. He must have had the benign religion his father taught in mind.

The war, which brought suffering, would 'stimulate the growth of our virtues' - suffering as a necessary condition of spiritual progress. Very much the kind of thing Voysey's father had said.

To turn now, briefly, to matters of design. While mediaeval craftsmen had understood 'the spiritual origin of nature', we had lost our way. If only we could approach nature with the humility of our forebears, our work would remain 'fresh in the hearts of men for generations to come, when our names may be forgotten'. How innocent Voysey sounds to us, for whom, as Yeats says the 'ceremony of innocence is drowned',

when he remarks: 'sincere thought and feeling is transmittable through things material, soul responds to soul . . . .'

Individuality is partly a diatribe against what Voysey called 'collectivism'. Individuality had to be cherished as the state had become all-powerful. The idea of individual responsiblity had to be fostered. The Edwardian vogue for the revival of the architectural style known as 'English Renaissance' - the style of Inigo Jones, Wren, Gibbs, and the style which was adopted by Lutyens was, according to Voysey, a manifestation of the collectivist spirit - the herd instinct driving people to follow fashion. The objection to Renaissance architecture is, obviously, Ruskinian. Our public buildings built in the neo-Renaissance manner were 'silent, dead, soulless piles of mortifying insincerity'.

This strange, sometimes bitter, book ends with the prediction that the outcome of the war will be to 'force men to distinguish more clearly between intellectual and spiritual culture, and thus to encourage the latter and . . . strengthen and sustain individuality'. Voysey's prognosis was wrong. Two decades later Europe was to see the apparent triumph of what Auden called 'collective man'.

10. House for the writer Julian Sturgis, at Puttenham, the Hog's Back, near Guildford, 1896.
Dekorative Kunst, V, 1897.
Known variously as Merlshanger, Wancote and Grey Friars - its present name, this was probably the most widely illustrated of Voysey's houses in contemporary publications.

11. Design originally for a wallpaper frieze c.1893. *The Studio*, I, September, 1893.
The design was known as 'The Minstrel' in its wallpaper version; as a woven fabric, produced by Alexander Morton & Co., it was known as 'The Pilgrim' (see Linda Parry, *Textiles of the Arts and Crafts Movement*, 1988, where a portion of the design is reproduced in colour).

Voysey's Decoration

Voysey started producing wallpaper and textile designs soon after he went into practice on his own in 1881. Trade was generally poor. Architectural commissions would have been hard to get, especially by an untried young architect. He probably turned to designing decoration in order to survive.

Voysey had learned the 'mechanical part' of decorative design in Seddon's office in particular - how to devise original motifs based upon plant drawings. He would also have learned the various forms of putting motifs into repeat. The acquisition of these skills would not have been taxing for anyone versed in applied geometry. During his time in Seddon's office Voysey was asked to paint a mural of angelic figures in one of his churches. It is difficult to imagine any such mural not incorporating decorative motifs. Voysey always had a penchant for angels. His simple, almost naive, figures would have been well suited to a mediaevalizing building.

Voysey learned little about decorative design from George Devey. For, fine draughtsman that he was, there is no evidence that he was accomplished in decorative design. Similarly, Snell could have had no part in Voysey's education in decorative design.

Arthur Heygate Mackmurdo, 1851-1942 and The Century Guild

It was A.H. Mackmurdo who first encouraged Voysey to develop a sideline in decorative design. Mackmurdo, also an architect, designed textiles for The Century Guild - an idealistic Morrisian association of designers - of which he had been a founder member in 1882. The guild aimed 'to render all branches of art the sphere no longer of the tradesman but the artist'. The writer and designer Aymer Vallance, 1862-1943, in 'Mr. Arthur H. Mackmurdo and the Century Guild', *The Studio*, April 1899, recalled that Voysey, while never a member, was in close contact with the guild for a number of years. Like other designers, he had resorted to it for 'advice, encouragement and sympathy'. Very likely, Mackmurdo would have given Voysey advice on the requirement of textile and wallpapers manufacturers. In 1883, Voysey sold his first wallpaper designs. The earliest Voysey decorative design in the RIBA Drawings Collection, however, dates from about 1887.

Mackmurdo is an interesting figure. His first essays in building reveal that he was stumbling towards the radical architectural position at which Voysey was actually to arrive. Mackmurdo, Vallance declared, had emancipated himself from 'prim Neo-Gothic artificiality'. Pevsner wrote that Mackmurdo's work was more original and more adventurous than that of any British architect during the decade 1880-1890 - 'which is tantamount to saying the work of any European architect'. While Pevsner may have been inclined to over-stress Mackmurdo's significance, it is evident that he is worthy of a more extended study than he has yet been accorded - if only because he was the pivot around which the Century Guild revolved. Other guild members include Selwyn Image, 1849-1930, a devout Ruskinian and a poet, who had relinquished holy orders in 1883. Image became Master of the Art Workers' Guild in 1900 and was Slade Professor at Oxford from 1910-1916. There was also Herbert Horne, 1864-1916, who had become Mackmurdo's pupil in 1883 and his partner in 1885. He retired at the age of thirty-six to Florence and bequeathed his collection and his house to the city.

Almost certainly, the most memorable achievement of the Century Guild was the publishing of *The Hobby Horse*, a periodical which propagated its ideals, published between 1884 and 1891. It was sophisticated in both graphic and literary terms.

Volume III of *The Hobby Horse*, which was published in 1888, contains facsimiles of the work of 16th century Florentine printers. An interest in any aspect of typography was remarkable in the 1880s. Contemporary typography was all too often coarse and ugly. *The Hobby Horse* was a notable exception. It is said that William Morris was inspired to set up his Kelmscott Press after encountering the elegant and urbane *Hobby Horse*.

The members of the Century Guild circle were aesthetes, in the sense in which the word is especially associated with the eighteen-eighties - when the writings of Walter Pater, or Matthew Arnold were at their most influential. Beauty was cultivated as a substitute for God. The Century Guild was Ruskinian in the manner of *Fors Clavigera*. 'Fors', as it became known, was addressed to the 'workmen and labourers of Great Britain'. It was entirely written by Ruskin and is filled with his invectives against industrialization - its despoilment of the earth and its degrading of humanity. Voysey moved, in the 1880s, in the Century Guild circle, but significantly he never joined the guild. While he could wring his hands at the ills of his time, he had a deep dislike of anything which savoured of socialism - Morrisian socialism included. Although he did not specifically attack socialism in *Individuality*, it is clear that he saw it as a manifestation of his hated 'collectivism'.

Whatever influence Seddon or Mackmurdo had upon Voysey as a decorative designer, it is essential to take into account the fact that he grew up at a time when there was a very great deal of interest taken in decoration. By the time he joined Seddon's office in 1873 a considerable literature on decoration, as well as many magnificent pattern books, existed. Pugin's *Glossary of Ecclesiastical Ornament*, 1844 and his *Floriated Ornaments*, 1849, have already been cited. Following in Pugin's wake, there was a widespread belief that decoration should carry a meaning - symbolic or didactic. The ultimate expression of 'didactic' decoration can be seen in the University Museum, Oxford, which was under construction in the late 1850s. It was designed by the Dublin partnership Deane and Woodward, under the influence, though not with the entire approval, of Ruskin. Here capitals, carved into the forms of native British flora and fauna, were intended to educate the townspeople and the students of Oxford in the ways of nature.

12. Arthur Heygate Mackmurdo.
Design for a cretonne, 1880.
The Studio, XVI, April, 1899.

Ornament books advocating natural forms as models for decoration abounded. The subject became known as 'art botany'. The Scottish painter William Dyce, 1806-64, Director of the Government School of Design, at Somerset House, in the early 1840s, published a teaching manual - *The Drawing Book of the Government School of Design*, 1842-3, which explained the way in which more or less naturalistic plant drawings could be arranged ornamentally. Although, it is hardly necessary to remark, ornament derived from plant forms is of the utmost antiquity, nineteenth century designers were to become fixated with the idea of nature as the supreme inventor of form. Natural forms - of a complexity and diversity beyond human imagining - reassured many people, during a time when faith was in crisis, that God might yet exist as a Supreme Designer. Lip service might be paid to conventional religion - as Ruskin often did - but an undertow of pantheism can be detected in much nineteenth-century thought. One senses this, too, in Voysey's love of nature.

There were many pattern books illustrating plant-based decorative design - besides Pugin's *Floriated Design* - which Voysey could have been influenced by during his formative years. Among these were: Owen Jones's *Grammar of Ornament*, 1856, the final chapter of which is devoted to botanical illustrations which were intended as an inspiration for ornamental designers; there were also Christopher Dresser's books; F. Edward Hulme's *Plant Form*, 1868; and Richard Redgrave's *Manual of Design*, 1876, published by the South Kensington Museum, which set out the approved method of generating plant-based decoration. However, the architect J.K. Colling's *Art Foliage*,

1865, was the standard work used by Gothic Revival architects - if Colling's design is a little too mechanical for our taste, *Art Foliage* is a very serviceable pattern book. Like Pugin's books, one would have expected to find it among the reference works in Seddon's office.

Voysey, in his interview in *The Studio*, of September, 1893, described his attitude towards nature as a source of inspiration:

'To go to Nature is, of course, to approach the fountain-head, but a literal transcript will not result in good ornament; before a living plant a man must go through an elaborate process of selection and analysis, and think of the balance, repetition and many of the qualities of design, thereby calling his individual taste into play and adding a human interest to his work. If he does that, although he has gone directly to Nature, his work will not resemble (that of) any of his predecessors, he has become an inventor.'

The 'elaborate process of selection and analysis' of which Voysey spoke - 'conventionalizing' was the contemporary term, where we would probably use 'stylizing' - had been, by 1893, taught to two generations of designers. The rationale of conventional decorative design, which was practised by Pugin, Owen Jones or Richard Redgrave, had become part of the studio folklore of designers. It was, like some of the

13. Proposed house for C.S. Loch, at Oxshott, Surrey, 1898.
The Studio, XVI, April, 1899.
Voysey used bays in a number of his houses at around this time of which Broadleys, Lake Windermere, 1898, is the best known example.

ideas of the Modern Movement, accepted quite uncritically. The cult of conventional design had its origins in the 1840s when intensive studies of mediaeval and, to a lesser extent, oriental decoration were initiated. Owen Jones, in *The Grammar of Ornament*, 1856, in proposition 13, (the propositions were axioms of good taste), stated that in decoration only conventional representations of 'flowers or other natural objects' which were 'sufficiently suggestive to convey the intended image to the mind' should be used. Thus rule was 'universally obeyed in the best periods of Art', and 'violated only when art declines'.

Voysey, of course, was part of a movement in architecture - a very vigorous one. He was similarly part of a movement in decorative design - the members of which had sought to raise national standards. Lewis F. Day, in 'The Art of William Morris', the Easter Art Annual, *The Art-Journal*, 1899, described this movement, with reference to Morris, of course. But his account remains one of the best summaries of the sequence of events:

'Morris was born just at the right moment: the way was prepared for him. Walter Scott, without really appreciating Gothic art, had called popular attention to its romance. Rickman had long since 'discriminated' the style of English Architecture. Pugin had established his *True Principles of Gothic Architecture* and was designing all manner of mediaeval furniture; and by the time (Morris) came to take any heed of art, Gothic architecture was the fashion. Shaw (presumably Henry Shaw - author of *The Encyclopaedia of Ornament*, 1842, and *Dresses and Decoration of the Middle Ages*, 1843) and others had published books on mediaeval antiquities and Viollet-le-Duc his famous dictionary; even Owen Jones, the orientalist, had cleared the ground, by creating a reaction of taste against mere naturalism pretending to be design. Fergusson, (James Fergusson, the architect and historian), Freeman, (presumably Edward A. Freeman, the authority on mediaeval architecture), Semper, (Gottfried Semper, the German architect and theorist), Wornum, (Ralph Nicholson Wornum, Keeper of the National Gallery, who had published *Analysis*

of Ornament in 1856) Digby Wyatt, (Matthew Digby Wyatt, a major architect, with an interest in decoration) and above all, Ruskin, had been writing about art until people were beginning to listen. Men like William Burges and E.W. Godwin were hard at work already: there was reaction in the air: the times were ready for the man - the man was William Morris.'

Among Voysey's own generation the following designers continued to advance the art of decoration: Charles Harrrison Townsend, 1851-1928, the architect of the Whitechapel Art Gallery and the Horniman Museum; George Heywood Sumner, 1853-1940, historian and designer; Arthur Silver, 1853-1896, founder of the successful Silver Studio; George C. Haité, 1855-1924, decorative designer and illustrator - he was one of the first illustrators employed by *The Strand Magazine*; Harry Napper, 1860-1940, who became manager of the Silver Studio after Arthur's death; May Morris, 1862-1938, William Morris's younger daughter and a leading embroiderer; Henry Wilson, 1864-1934, a leading arts and crafts architect; M.H. Baillie Scott, 1865-1945, whose influence on domestic architecture possibly equalled Voysey's; and Lindsay Butterfield, 1869-1948, who was, together with Voysey, among the most successful decorative designers of the era. All, like Voysey it is hardly necessary to add, were skilled in transforming natural forms into decoration.

From the earlier generation, two designers are likely to have had a great influence on Voysey. These were Walter Crane and Lewis F. Day. Lewis Foreman Day, 1845-1910, is probably best known today for his textbooks on decoration - they have yet to be bettered and remain in regular use. The first of these was *Instances of Necessary Art*, 1880. Day was also an excellent designer himself. He was a founder member of the Arts and Crafts Exhibition Society in 1887. Walter Crane, 1845-1915, the first president of the Arts and Crafts Exhibition Society, was successful as both an illustrator - he was a pioneer of illustration for children - and as a decorative designer. His textbooks, however, did not appear until a decade and a half after Voysey had established himself as a decorative designer. Voysey's pictorial textiles and wallpapers suggest, very strongly, the influence of Crane. Crane had, much earlier than Voysey, in 'Sing a Song of Sixpence', a wallpaper for Jeffrey & Co of 1875, demonstrated the role of pictorial design in brightening the nursery and stimulating the minds of the very young.

In its themes and its components - its elements - Voysey's decoration is typical of the 1880s and 1890s. Voysey's decorative ideas, almost all of them, were formed during these two decades. Like other Arts and Crafts designers, he did not seek to break free of tradition. He did, however, discourage dependency upon past styles for inspiration. In *Individuality*, 1915, he wrote that 'if we cast behind us all preconceived styles, our work will still possess a style, but it will be a living, natural and true expression of modern needs and ideals: not an insincere imitation of other nations and other times'.

Like so many of his contemporaries, Voysey looked forward to the revitalization of rural life and society. The importance of reviving the life of the countryside - as an antidote to the ravages wrought by industrialization - is, of course, highly explicit in the writings of Ruskin and Morris. Their views also relate, in part, to the long-standing pastoral traditions of British literature and art which is exemplified in the writings of Blake, Coleridge, or Wordsworth, and in those of an architect, turned writer, Thomas Hardy. It is also manifest in the paintings of such artists as Richard Wilson, Constable and Palmer.

Voysey's decorative *oeuvre* fits comfortably into the niche labelled 'Arts and Crafts'. To say so is in no way to underestimate his achievement - for he was as accomplished a designer of wallpapers and textiles as any of his contemporaries. Voysey's decoration was, in a very real sense, archetypically Arts and Crafts. It certainly answered Morris's call that decoration should be - 'something that will not drive us into unrest or into callowness; something which reminds us of life beyond itself . . . '. 'Life beyond itself'? - surely Morris meant the life of the fields and the hedgerows. Nature was seen as a soothing, healing, agent. Morris's era, Voysey's era, was as preoccupied with the problem of isolation - alienation - in society as our

own. Decorative design was seen as having a therapeutic role to play.

An aspect of Voysey's decoration which will strike anyone who compares it with the generality of late nineteenth century design, is that it is unlaboured. There is an intentional lack of mechanical preciseness, an informality, which one does not find in, for example, the decoration of Morris, Day or Crane. The same qualities, though impossible to be entirely specific about, are to be found in Voysey's colour schemes. During the 1850s an elaborate 'science of colour harmony' had been developed - its complex rules account for twenty-one of the 37 propositions in *The Grammar of Ornament* (in a popular form, Dresser re-stated them in Cassell's *The Technical Educater*, 1870-72). The rules of colour harmony were taught to design students for many years. Voysey, evidently an intuitive colourist, ignored the strictures of this inhibiting pseudo-science. His colouring is invariably pleasing. It was widely imitated - M.H. Baillie Scott's colour schemes being a case in point.

Voysey is not a curious anomaly - the proto-modern born before his time, although Modernists were all too-inclined to claim him for themselves. His work seems to hint at a coming, more perfect, world. We feel a certain nostalgia for the age which brought forth such visions. But the visions were shattered beyond repair by the unspeakable events of the Great War.

'Let every bit of ornament speak to us of bright and healthy thought', wrote Voysey in 'Ideas in Things', 1909. Such idealism - essentially the idealism of Plato, (although there is no shred of evidence that Voysey ever read Plato) - seems altogether too simplistic for us to take entirely seriously now. But it is part and parcel of Voysey. The Voysey who is so like, yet so unlike, his contemporaries. His work is both naive and sophisticated, childlike and wise.

Yeats in a well-known four-line poem of 1933, dedicated to the artist Edmund Dulac - 'The Nineteenth Century and After' - mourned the century's passing and likened it to 'a great song'. Voysey, with his delicacy of expression, his poetic sensibility, was part of that great song.

Selected list of surviving buildings

1888 The Cottage, Station Road, Bishop's Itchington, Warwick, for M.H. Lakin.

1890 Walnut Tree Farm, (now Bannut Farm House), Castlemorton, near Malvern, Hereford and Worcester, for R.H. Cazalet.

1891 Studio at 17, St Dunstan's Road, London, W 6, for W.E.F. Britten.

1891 14, South Parade, Bedford Park, London, W 4, for J.W. Foster.

1891-2 Nos. 14 and 16, Hans Road, London, SW 3, for Archibald Grove.

1893 Perrycroft, Jubilee Drive, Colwall, near Malvern, Hereford and Worcester, for J.W. Wilson, M.P.

1895 Annesley Lodge, Platt's Lane, Hampstead, NW 3, for his father, Rev Charles Voysey.

1896 Grey Friars, Hog's Back, near Guildford, Surrey, for Julian Sturgis.

1897 Norney Grange, Shackleford, near Godalming, Surrey, for Rev W. Leighton Crane.

1897 New Place, Farnham Lane, Haslemere, Surrey, for A.M. Stedman, later Sir Algernon Methuen.

1898 Broadleys, Gillhead, near Cartmel Fell, Lake Windermere, Cumbria, for A. Currer Briggs.

1899 Spade House, Radnor Cliff Crescent, Sandgate, Folkestone, Kent, for H.G. Wells.

1899 The Orchard, Shire Lane, Chorley Wood, Hertfordshire, for his family.

1900 Prior's Garth, Puttenham, Surrey, for F.H. Chambers. Now a school - numerous modifications.

1902 Wallpaper factory, Barley Mow Passage, Chiswick, W 4, for Sanderson & Sons. Now leased as separate offices and workshops.

1902 Vodin, now Little Court, Old Woking Road, Pyrford, Surrey, for F. Walters.

1903 Ty Bronna, St Fagan's Road, Fairwater, near Cardiff, South Glamoragan, Wales, for W. Hastings Watson.

1903 Tilehurst, 10, Grange Road, Bushey, Hertfordshire, for Miss Somers.

1904-5 Institute and houses, Whitwood, near Normanton, Yorkshire, for Henry Briggs & Son. The Institute is now a public house - The Rising Sun.

1905 The Homestead, Second Avenue, corner of Holland Road, Frinton-on-Sea, Essex, for S.C. Turner.

1906-7 Littleholme, Upper Guildown Road, Guildford, Surrey, for G. Muntzer.

1911 House in Malone Road, Belfast, Northern Ireland, for Robert Hetherington.

1919-20 War memorials at Malvern Wells and Potter's Bar.

Manufacturers of textiles, carpets and wallpapers to whom Voysey supplied designs:

G.P. & J. Baker	Newman, Smith, Newman
Donald Brothers	Samson Brothers
D'Oyly	Sanderson
Essex	H.M. Southwell
William Foxton	Harold Speed
T. Ginzkey (of Maffersdorf, Austria)	Stead McAlpine
Jeffery	Tomkinson & Adam
A.H. Lee	Templeton
Lightbown, Aspinall	J.W. & C. Ward
Line & Son	Wm. Woollams & Company
Alexander Morton, Morton Sundour	Yates
Muntzer	

Voysey is also believed to have designed for the following shops:

Liberty   Wylie & Lochead   Storry

— Bibliography —

Books

Adams, Maurice B., *Modern Cottage Architecture, illustrated from works of well-known architects*, London 1904

Allibone, Jill, *George Devey*, Cambridge 1990

Arts and Crafts Essays by Members of the Arts and Crafts Exhibition Society. With a preface by William Morris, London 1893

Banham, Reyner, *Theory and Design in the First Machine Age*, London 1960 (new edn 1980)

Brandon-Jones, John, *C.F.A. Voysey: a Memoir*, London, 1957

Cassou, Jean, Langui, Emile, and Pevsner, Nikolaus, *The Sources of Modern Art*, London 1962 (German edn, Munich 1961)

Colling, James Kellaway, *Art Foliage for Sculpture and Decoration*, London 1865

Crane, Walter, *William Morris to Whistler: Papers and Addresses on Art and Craft and the Commonweal . . . with illustrations from drawings by the author and other sources*, London 1911
    See 'The English Revival in Modern Decorative Art'

Cloag, John, *The English Tradition in Design*, London 1947

Crook, J. Mordaunt, *The Dilemma of Style: Architectural Ideas from the Picturesque to the Post-Modern*, London 1987

Davey, Peter, *Arts and Crafts Architecture: The Search for Earthly Paradise*, London 1980

Durant, Stuart, *Ornament: A Survey of Decoration since 1830*, London 1986

Elder-Duncan, J.H., *Country Cottages and Week-End Homes*, London 1906

Evans, Joan, *Pattern: A Study of Ornament in Western Europe, 1180-1900*, Oxford 1931 & New York 1975

Farr, Dennis, *English Art, 1870-1940*, Oxford, 1978

Ferriday, Peter (editor), *Victorian Architecture . . . with an introduction by John Betjeman*, London 1968
    See Brandon-Jones, John, 'C.F.A. Voysey'

Gebhard, David, *Charles F.A. Voysey: Architect*, Los Angeles 1975

Girouard, Mark, *Sweetness and Light: The Queen Anne Movement, 1860-1900*, Oxford 1977

Girouard, Mark, *The Victorian Country House*, Oxford 1971

Gloag, John, *The English Tradition in Design*, London 1947

Holme, Charles, *Modern British Domestic Architecture and Decoration*, London 1901

Jones, Owen, *The Grammar of Ornament*, London 1856

Jones, Owen, *The Leading Principles in the Composition of Ornament of Every Period*, London n.d.

Macartney, Mervyn E. (editor) *Recent English Domestic Architecture*, London 1911

McGrath, Raymond, *Twentieth-Century Houses*, London 1934

Marriott, Charles, *Modern English Architecture*, London 1924

Morris, William, *News from Nowhere*, London, 1890

Morris, William, *Some Hints on Pattern Designing*, London 1899

Muthesius, Hermann, *Das Englische Haus*, Berlin, this edition, 1908-1911

Muthesius, Hermann, *Landhaus und Garten . . .*, Munich 1910 (first edn, 1907)

Muthesius, Hermann, *Das Moderne Landhaus und seine innere Austattung*, Munich 1905

Pevsner, Nikolaus, *Pioneers of the Modern Movement: From William Morris to Walter Gropius*, London 1936 (reprinted as *Pioneers of Modern Design*, New York, 1949)

Pevsner, Nikolaus, *Studies in Art, Architecture and Design*, vol 2 *Victorian and After*, London 1968
    See 'C.F.A. Voysey', which first appeared in *Elseviers Mandschrift*, May 1940; translated by Caroline Doggart and revised by Nicolas Pevsner. *See also* 'A.H. Mackmurdo', which first appeared in *The Architectural Review*, LXXXIII, 1938

Pugin, A.W.N., *Contrasts*, London 1841 (first edn 1836)

Pugin, A.W.N., *Floriated Ornament*, London 1849

Pugin, A.W.N., *Glossary of Ecclesiastical Ornament and Costume*, London 1844

Pugin, A.W.N., *Gothic Furniture in the Style of the Fifteenth Century*, London 1835

Ruskin, John, *Diaries* (ed. by Joan Evans and John Howard Whitehouse, 3 vols), Oxford 1956-59

Ruskin, John, *Fors Clavigera*, Orpington, 1871-84

Ruskin, John, *The Seven Lamps of Architecture*, London 1849

Ruskin, John, *The Stones of Venice*, London 1852-53

Redgrave, Richard, *Manual of Design*, London n.d. [1876]

Schmutzler, Robert, *Art Nouveau*, London 1964 (German edn, Stuttgart 1962)

Simpson, Duncan, *C.F.A. Voysey: An Architect of Individuality. With a Preface by Sir James Richards*, London 1979. (Simpson organized the 1978 Voysey exhibition in Brighton. *See* Catalogues: Brandon-Jones, John, and others)

Sparrow, Walter Shaw (editor), *The British Home of Today: A Book of Modern Domestic Architecture and the Applied Arts*, London 1904

Sugden, Alan Victor, and Edmundson, John Ludlam, *A History of British Wallpaper, 1509-1914*, London n.d. [1925]

Thompson, Paul, *William Butterfield*, London 1971

Townsend, W.G. Paulson, *Modern Decorative Art in England*, London 1922

Voysey, Charles, *Theism: The Religion of Common Sense*, London, [this edn 1896]

Voysey, C.F.A., ' "Ideas in Things", two lectures in The Arts Connected with Building' *Lectures on Craftsmanship and Design . . .*, (Edited by T. Raffles Davison), London 1909

Voysey, C.F.A., *Individuality*, London 1915 (Reprinted Shaftesbury,1986)

Voysey, C.F.A., *Reason as a Basis for Art*, London 1906

Weaver, Lawrence (editor), *Small Country Houses of Today*, London n.d. [1910]

Wilmott, Ernest, *English House Design: A Review . . .*, London 1911

Selected Articles

Anon. (possibly Gleeson White) 'An interview with Mr. Charles F. Annesley Voysey, architect and designer', *The Studio*, I, 1893, 231-37

Henry Van de Velde, 'Artistic Wallpapers', *Emulation*, XVIII, Brussels, 1893, 150-51

Henry Van de Velde, 'Essex and Co's Westminster Wallpapers', *L'Art Moderne*, XIV, Brussels, 1894, 253-54

Anon., 'Art in Decoration and Design', *The Builder*, LXVIII, 1895, 151

E.B.S., 'Some Recent Designs by Mr. C.F.A. Voysey', *The Studio*, VII, 1896, 218-19

'G', 'The Revival of English Domestic Architecture: The Work of Mr. C.F.A. Voysey', *The Studio*, XI, 1897, 16-25

Anon., (possibly Herbert Muthesius or P.G. Konody), 'C.F.A. Voysey', *Dekorative Kunst*, I, Munich, 1897, 241-80

Horace Townsend, 'Notes on Country and Suburban Houses designed by C.F.A. Voysey', *The Studio*, XVI, 1899, 157-64

Aymer Vallance, 'British Decorative Art in 1899 and the Arts and Crafts Exhibition', *The Studio*, XVIII, 1899, 38-49

M.P. Verneuil, 'Le papier-peint à l'exposition', *Art et Décoration*, VIII, Paris, 1900, 83-90

Anon., 'The Arts and Crafts Exhibition at the New Gallery', *The Studio*, XXXVIII 1903, 28, 179

Aymer Vallence, 'Some recent work by Mr. C.F.A. Voysey', *The Studio*, XXXI, 1904, 127-34

Anon., 'Some recent designs for domestic architecture', *The Studio*, XXXIV, 1905, 151-52

P.G. Konody, 'C.F.A. Voyseys neuere arbeiten', *Dekorative Kunst*, XIV, Munich, 1906, 193-98

Paul Klopfer, 'Voysey's Architektur-Idyllen', *Moderne Bauformen*, IX, Stuttgart, 1910,141-48

Halsey, Ricardo, a review of *Individuality* by C.F.A. Voysey, *RIBA Journal*, XXII, 1915, 336

Anon., 'C.F.A. Voysey, the Man and his Work', *The Architect & Building News*, CXVII, 1927, (in five parts, beginning p.133)

John Betjeman, 'Charles Francis Annesley Voysey, the architect of individualism', *The Architectural Review*, LXX, 1931, 93-96

H.M. Fletcher, 'The Work of C.F.A. Voysey', review of an exhibition at the Batsford Gallery, *RIBA Journal*, XXXVIII, 1931, 763-64

H.Fürst, 'The Exhibition of the Work of C.F.A. Voysey at the Batsford Gallery', *Apollo*, XIV, 1931, 245

The Editor, 'Royal Gold Medallist', *RIBA Journal*, XLVII, 1940

Anon., 'C.F.A. Voysey', *The Architect & Building News*, CLXI, 1940, 1996-97

John Betjeman, 'C.F.A. Voysey', *Architect's Journal*, XCI, 1940, 234-35

The Editor, 'The Royal Gold Medal Award to Mr. C.F.A. Voysey', *The Builder*, CLIX, 1940, 237

John Summerson, 'Mr Voysey: Veteran Gold Medallist', *The Listener*, XXIII, 1940, 479-80

John Betjeman, 'C.F.A. Voysey', *Architectural Forum*, LXII, New York, 1940, 348-49

J.M. Richards, obituary, *Architectural Review*, LXXXIX, 1941, 112-13

Nikolaus Pevsner, 'Charles F. Annesley Voysey, 1857-1941', *The Architectural Review*, LXXXIX, 1941, 112-13

Howard Robinson & Noel D. Sheffield, obituary, *RIBA Journal*, XLVIII, 1941, 88

Anon., obituary, *Architect's Journal*, XCIII, 1941, 124

Robert Donat, 'Uncle Charles . . .', *Architect's Journal*, XCIII, 1941, 193-94

John Betjeman, 'C.F.A. Voysey', *Architect's Journal*, XCIII, 1941, 257-58

John Brandon-Jones, 'An Architect's Letters to his Client', *Architect and Building News*, CXCV, 1949, 494-98

Martin S. Briggs, 'Voysey and Blomfield, a study in Contrast', *The Builder*, CLXXVI, 1949

Peter Floud, 'Voysey Wallpaper', *Penrose Annual*, LII, 1958, 10-14

Margaret Richardson, 'Wallpapers by C.F.A. Voysey', *RIBA Journal*, LXXII, 1965, 399-403

John Brandon-Jones, 'Architects and the Art Worker's Guild', *Journal of the Royal Society of Arts*, CXXI, 1973, 192-203

Louis Hellman, 'Voysey in Wonderland', *Building Design*, 169, 28 September 1973, 18-22

Catalogues

Architect-Designers, Pugin to Mackintosh, London 1981

Arts and Crafts Exhibition Society. *Catalogue of the First Exhibition*. London 1888 (and later catalogues)

Arts Décoratifs de Grande-Bretagne et d'Irlande, London, 1914

Brandon-Jones, John, and others, *C.F.A. Voysey: Architect and Designer, 1857-1941*, Brighton 1978

Exhibition of British Design for Surface Decoration, London 1915 (The Board of Trade)

Floud, Peter (editor), *Exhibition of Victorian and Edwardian Decorative Arts*, London 1952 (*See* Section S: C.F.A. Voysey)

Catalogue of A.H. Mackmurdo and the Century Guild Collection, London 1967

Gebhard, David, *Charles F. A. Voysey*. Santa Barbara, California 1970

Great British Architects, London 1981, with an introduction by Sir John Summerson. (Catalogue of an exhibition at the Architectural Association. The architects are: Chambers, Searles, Pugin, Chas. Barry, Voysey and Rickards)

Oman, Charles C. and Hamilton, Jean, *Wallpaper: A History and Illustrated Catalogue of the Collection at the Victoria and Albert Museum*, London, 1983

Parry, Linda, *Textiles of the Arts and Crafts Movement*, London 1988

Physick, John, and Darby, Michael, '*Marble Halls*': *Drawings and Models for Victorian Secular Buildings*, London 1973

Les Sources du XXe Siècle: Les Arts en Europe de 1884 à 1914, Paris 1960

Darby, Michael, *John Pollard Seddon: Catalogues of Architectural Drawings in the Victoria and Albert Museum*, London 1983

Selz, Peter, and Constantine, Mildred, *Art Nouveau: Art & Design at the Turn of the Century*, New York, 1959

Summary Catalogue of Textile Designs, 1840-1985, in the Victoria and Albert Museum, microfiche, London 1988

Symonds, Joanna, *C.F.A. Voysey: Catalogue of the Drawings Collection of the Royal Institute of British Architects*, London 1975

Victorian Church Art, London 1971

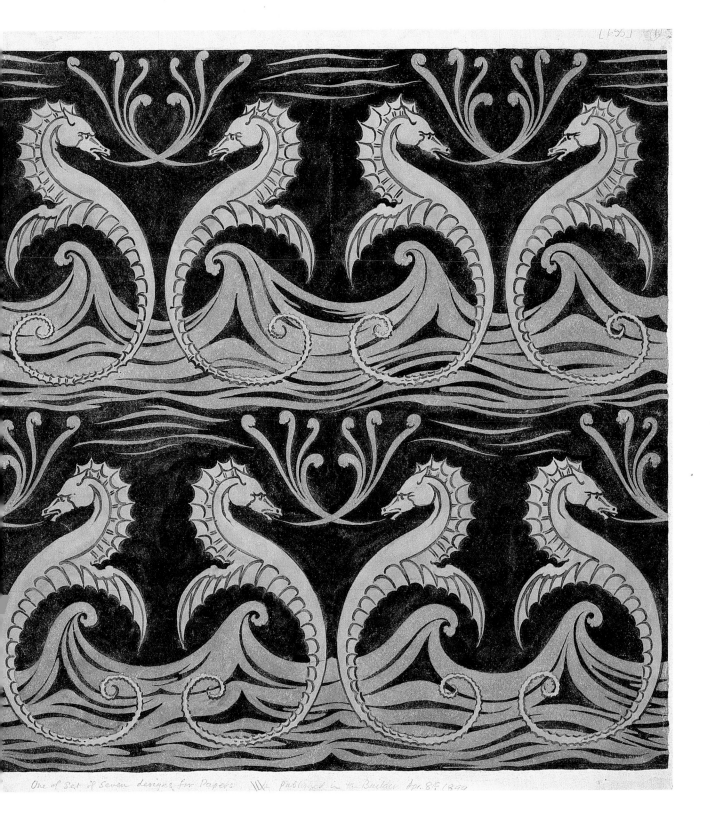

One of Set of Seven designs for Paper: XX published in the Builder Apr 8th 1890

1. Design for a wallpaper, or possibly a woven silk. c. 1887 [655]
445x420
Illustrated in *The Builder*, LXXVI, 1899

Voysey began producing decorative designs shortly after he had set up his own practice in 1882.
This is the earliest example in the RIBA Drawings Collection. Sea creatures and the sea itself
fascinated Voysey's contemporaries - William Burges's bedroom in Melbury Road in West London
was decorated with symbols of the sea

2. Design for a textile. c. 1888 [656]
    Noted ' "For 54" cloth'
    780x560
    Illustrated in Cassou, Langui and Pevsner, *The Sources of Modern Art*, 1962, and Tschudi Madsen, *Art Nouveau*, 1967

    There is an affinity in the undulating forms of the lilies - depicted with no great botanical exact-itude - and certain decorative work of Walter Crane, 1845-1915, or Heywood Samner, 1853-1940. A.H. Mackmurdo, Voysey's friend, used similarly undulating forms in his designs, which were inspired by the work of William Blake

3. Design for a wallpaper or textile. April, 1889 [657]
Inscribed verso 'Arts & Crafts', presumably indicating that the design was exhibited at the Arts and Crafts Exhibition Society, founded in 1888
490x410
Illustrated in Durant, *Ornament: A Survey of Decoration since 1830*, 1986

Herbert Horne, a member of the Century Guild (see page 24), produced a design for block-printed cotton, 'The Angel with Trumpet' between 1884 and 1888 (see Linda Parry, *Textiles of the Arts and Crafts Movement*, 1988, p.43). Voysey's angelic figures bear a passing resemblance to Horne's, but the small silhouette devils - driven to flight by the angels - have come entirely from Voysey's own imagination. As a Theist, of course, Voysey would have had no belief in Hell (see page 11). Voysey once painted a mural of angels for Seddon, to whom he was articled in 1874 (see page 13)

35

4. Design for a wallpaper produced by Essex & Co. Dated in the RIBA Catalogue as 'pre-1899', but attributed, on stylistic grounds, to the late-1880s [863a]
Noted 'Vulture and lily symbols of purity' and in another hand 'probably pre-1889'
405x390
Illustrated in *The Builder*, LXXVI, 1899

Apparently an early design. Might the symbolism indicate an equilibrium between good and evil?

5. Design for a wallpaper or textile, called 'The Demon', 1889 [658]
430x300
Illustrated in *The Studio*, I, 1893

There seems to be no precedent for wallpapers, or textiles, incorporating depictions of diabolical figures - although in the 1870s, Christopher Dresser, 1834-1904, based designs on malevolent-looking Thai ballet masks. Voysey's devil, however, is based on the Renaissance version of the devil, which is itself based on the satyr of classical times

6. Design for a wallpaper, c. 1889 [not listed in RIBA Catalogue]
   396x381

   The presence of gilt indicates conclusively that this design was intended as a wallpaper. This design
   was possibly exhibited at the Arts and Crafts Society exhibition, as it is inscribed 'Arts and Crafts'
   on the verso. Fanciful creatures appear fairly frequently in the late nineteenth-century illustrations -
   Tenniel's Jabberwocky is a well-known example

7.   Design for a printed velvet called 'The Three Men of Gotham', c. 1889 [659]
Noted, in another hand, 'Finished 14/7/96'
555x725
Illustrated in *The Studio*, I, 1893

The story illustrated by this design is correctly called 'The Three Wise Men of Gotham'. Gotham is in Nottinghamshire, and the three wise men are said to have feigned madness to prevent King John establishing a right of way by coming through their village. The story appears in a sixteenth-century chapbook. Ancient ships of this kind appear in early illustrations by Walter Crane, and in paintings by E. Burne-Jones

8. Design for a wallpaper or textile called 'Claudea', April, 1890 [660]
Noted ' "Claudea", Southern Ocean'
510x450

Purely linear designs for textiles, or wallpapers, were unusual at this time. The design suggests that Voysey may have had a passing interest in Japanese decoration, although the vogue for Japanese design was passing by 1890. It is not known whether this design was actually produced

9.   Design for a wallpaper called 'Bushey'. Produced by Essex & Co, c. 1890 [661]
780x560
Illustrated in *The Studio*, III, 1894

This is the earliest of the designs in the RIBA Drawings Collection that is known to have been manufactured. Voysey produced many designs for Essex & Co, including its trademark (see page 18), some advertisements, and a house - not built ultimately according to his plans - for R.W. Essex, the managing director. The darker colouring of the ground (bottom left) presumably indicates how the design could be modified

10. Design for a wallpaper, c. 1890 [662]
    Noted 'Anaglypta' and 'Samson Brothers' which suggests that the design was actually sold
    555x375

    Even Voysey's simplest designs indicate that he had a strong feeling for outline - the Victorians
    spoke of the outline of a building as 'the sky blotch'. Voysey's buildings are always assertive in outline

11. Design for a wallpaper and carpet, c. 1890 [663]
   Noted in another hand on the verso is 'something like this sold to Line & Son for paper ditto ditto
   D'Oyly for carpet circa 1890'
   405x265

   Although the design, at first sight, appears to have little in common with the decorations of
   A.W.N. Pugin, it was Pugin who established in his *Glossary of Ecclesiastical Ornament*, 1844, how
   the simplest forms of ornament should be handled. Voysey, who admired Pugin, is likely to have
   known the work

12. Design for a workbox, c. 1893 [864]
    280x565
    Illustrated in *The Studio*, I, 1893

The box was exhibited at the Arts and Crafts exhibition of 1893. It was of inlaid sycamore. The male figure - sketching - may well be Voysey himself; the female figure - knitting? - is thus likely to be his wife

13. Design for a wallpaper frieze called 'Seagull', c. 1893 [666]
Noted on the verso is 'Frieze for "Seagull" design 1893'. Also noted is the fact that the watermark of the paper on which the design is executed is dated 1905. Voysey was in the habit of copying his own designs - the reason for the practice is not clear
475x565

The tree is obviously based on a sketch from nature. Like all his Arts and Crafts contemporaries, Voysey derived great inspiration from nature

14. Design for a wallpaper called 'Shallop', two colourways, c. 1893 [668]
780x560
This was redrawn in 1900. Illustrated in Peter Floud, 'The Wallpaper Designs of C.F.A. Voysey',
Penrose Annual, LII, 1958

The design is probably based on that illustrated in Plate 13. It is, however, possible that this design
is actually the earlier of the two. A shallop is a small open boat

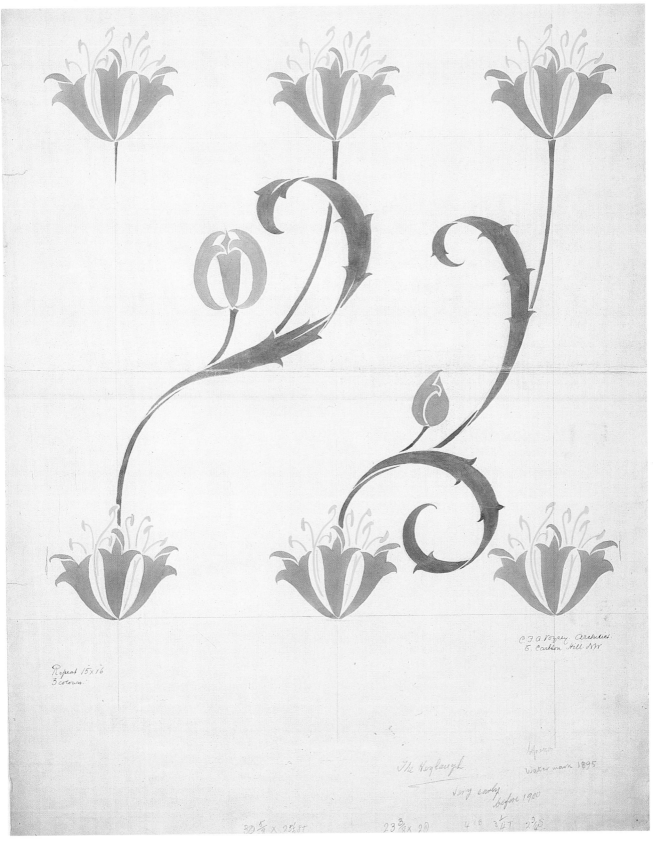

15. Design for a wallpaper called 'Heylaugh', c. 1895 [669]
Noted in a hand, not Voysey's, is 'The Heylaugh - very early, before 1900. Watermark 1895'
775x560

Heylaugh is obviously a modified spelling of Healaugh, the parish from which Voysey's father was dismissed for unorthodox preaching in 1869. The break in the rhythm of the formalized foliage would have the effect of creating a more complex overall visual texture. Voysey clearly understood - at an empirical level - the operations of *Gestalt* perception

47

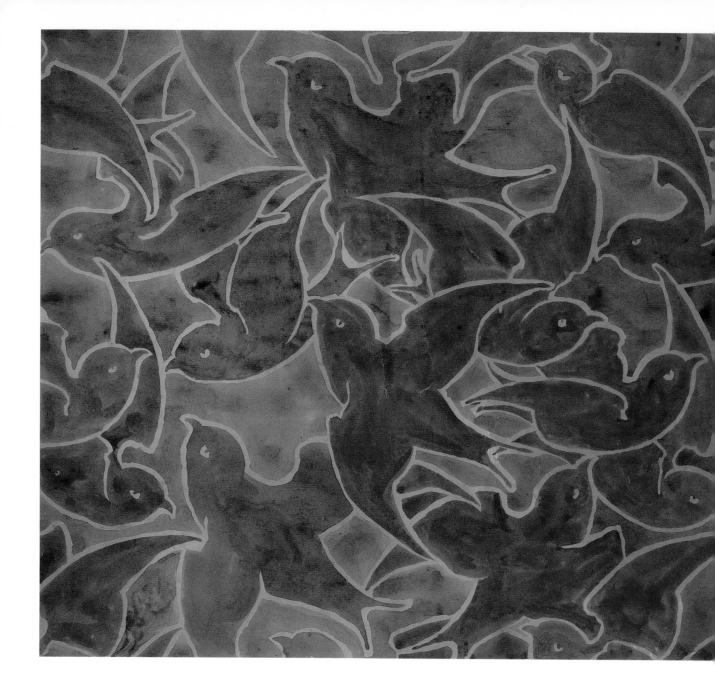

16. Design for a wallpaper, c. 1895 [822]
    Inscribed 'SX', signifying that the design was produced by or sold to Essex & Co
    320x370

    The design is undated, but is attributed, on stylistic grounds, to the mid-1890s. Voysey was particularly fond of outline birds - they appear in his design for the 1893 cover of *The Studio*. *The Studio* of July 1894 illustrated a design of interlocking birds by the Silver Studio quite close to this design - this was for a ceiling paper

17. Design for an embroidered bed quilt called
'Squire's Garden', 1896 [670]
Dated, in Voysey's hand, 'Jany. 1896'
780x510
A similar design exists in the Print Room,
the Victoria and Albert Museum

The quilt was embroidered by Mrs
Reynolds-Stephens, the sculptor's wife.
The design was subsequently reproduced as
a wallpaper. Walter Crane had made the
pictorial decorative design respectable. His
'Sing a Song of Sixpence', a nursery
wallpaper was produced by Jeffrey & Co in
1875; his 'The House that Jack Built' was
produced in 1886

18. Design for a wallpaper called 'The Callum', c. 1896 [671]
Noted verso 'The Callum very early wallpaper for Essex'
500x310
Illustrated in *The Studio*, VII, 1896, where it is called 'Mimosa'

With considerable economy, Voysey creates a design which is as satisfactory as a more complex, more laborious, design by Morris

19. Design for a wallpaper, c. 1896 [673]
Noted 'Essex'
440x420
Illustrated in Cassou, Langui and Pevsner, *The Sources of Modern Art*, 1962. A similar design, dated 1889, exists in the Print Room, the Victoria and Albert Museum

The water snake would appear to emanate entirely from Voysey's imagination. Underwater decorative themes were not uncommon in the 1890s. Designs by Hermann Obrist, 1862-1927, of embroideries inspired by sea creatures appeared in *The Studio*, IX, 1896. In 1899, the great German marine biologist Ernst Häckel, 1834-1919, began publishing his *Kunstformen der Natur* (Art Forms in Nature), which contained numerous illustrations of sea creatures as inspirations for designers. Hector Guimard's Parisian apartment block Castel Bérenger, 1894-1898, is decorated with sea themes

20. Design for a wallpaper and tapestry produced by Essex & Co in honour of Queen Victoria's Diamond Jubilee, 1897 [674]
940x805
Illustrated in *The Builder*, LXXVI, 1899, *Dekorative Kunst*, I, 1897

This design is among the most Pugin-like of Vosyey's decorative designs in the Drawings Collection of the RIBA. Voysey may have known Pugin's wallpapers from the Houses of Parliament. Like many designers who grew up during the period of the Gothic Revival, Voysey was interested in heraldry. The heart and the two birds establish this unmistakably as a Voysey design

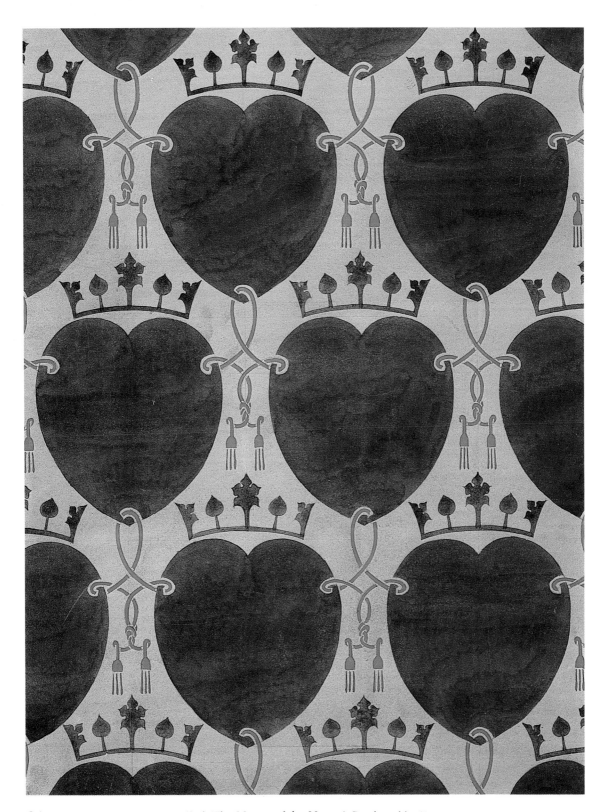

21. Design for a wallpaper called 'The Union of the Hearts'. Produced by Essex & Co. Watermark 1898 [675]
Noted on the verso is 'Produced by Essex & Co. Design for woven fabric to be sent to Arts & Crafts. SX [Essex]. AM [Alexander Morton]. J&M. J&A. Carpet for Tomkinsons'
510x340
Illustrated in *Good Furniture Magazine*, XXIII, 1924, Brandon-Jones and others, *C.F.A. Voysey: Architect and Designer, 1859-1941*, Brighton, 1978, Durant, *Ornament . . .*, 1986

The iconographical significance of this design is not known. The crown may link it to the Diamond Jubilee design (Plate 20). The heart was Voysey's personal symbol - the heart , of course, has a long history as a symbol of love, both secular and divine

22. Design for a wallpaper, or possibly a textile, called 'I Love Little Pussy'. Watermark '8' (1898? or 1908?). Attributed here on stylistic grounds to 1898 [839]
555x300

The reference to the well-known rhyme suggests that this design was intended for a nursery wallpaper. The cat is observing her prey - birds and rats. The Print Room of the Victoria and Albert Museum possesses a design for a textile illustrating a cat looking at a canary, dating from the 1920s. The design is called 'Let us Prey'

54

23. Design, possibly for a wallpaper, 1900 [676]
1005x390

Like such other nineteenth-century decorative
designers - Pugin, Owen Jones, Christopher
Dresser, Bruce Talbert or E.W. Godwin - Voysey
was skilled in achieving rich effects through the
simplest means. The organization of this design,
however, suggests the influence of William Morris

24. Design for a wallpaper and
textile, 1900 [678]
Noted is 'This has been
drawn up for Alex.
M[orton]. & Essex. May 28,
1900
390x340

Voysey had a particular fondness for bird motifs. Birds, as decoration, have a long history in
English design. There is a fine misericord of c. 1300 in Wells Cathedral the central feature of
which is a motif of identical birds facing each other. William Morris's early 'Trellis' wallpaper, 1864,
incorporates birds drawn by his friend Philip Webb. Selwyn Image of the Century Guild was also
fond of birds as motifs

25. Design for a wallpaper or textile called 'Alena', May, 1901 [685]
Noted in Voysey's hand is 'All the birds are repeats of this one' (referring to the bird with its feathers drawn in)
235x300

This is drawn on light tracing paper of the kind used by many nineteenth-century designers. This may be a sketch design. It was executed rapidly, and with great confidence, and shows Voysey's flowing, calligraphic, line

26. Design for a wallpaper frieze, c. 1902 [698]
Noted are details of the colouring
780x555

Drawn in pencil and chalk, this is presumably a preliminary design

58

This is
the who

27. Design for a carpet, dated 3 March 1903 [699]
Reproduced approximately the size of the original
Noted are details of the colouring
325x395

The motifs are intended to be reproduced on a square grid

28. Full-size working drawings of the 'River Rug', 1903 [706 . . .]
Noted: 'Quality', 'Coronation' verso. T. Ginzkey. Maffersdo(rf)'. With the working drawings is a
photograph of the whole design inscribed 'The River Mat. Drawings of this design Full-sized . . .
made & coloured by C.F.A. Voysey F.R.I.B.A. 73 St James St S.W.1. in his possession. Size of rug 8
feet by 4 feet. . . .'
2440x1220 approx
Illustrated in *Kunst und Kunsthandwerk*, VI, 1903

The rug was exhibited at the Arts and Crafts exhibition of 1903. It remained in the Voysey family
for many years and is now in a private collection. It would appear that Voysey intended to sell
copies of the design to amateur rug-makers. It would have taken a considerable time to complete

29. Detail of the 'River Rug', 1903. See Plate 28
315x640

When Voysey was working in George Devey's office in the early 1880s (see pages 15-17) he was sent to Ireland to prepare a rent-roll, possibly for the Earl of Kenmare. Voysey produced a book with pages of drawings of cottages, their inhabitants and livestock (see Allibone, *George Devey*). It is conceivable that the design was inspired by the Irish rent-book. Here, however, the scene is entirely from Voysey's imagination

30. Detail of the 'River Rug', 1903. See Plates 28 and 29

The bird called the Halcyon, concerning which the old fable runs, that she was the daughter of Aeolus & mourning in her youth for the lost husband was winged by Divine power, & now flies over the sea, seeking him whom she could not find.
Halcyone was the daughter of the Winds. Kingfisher
The bird known as the Halcyon is ~~~~ they ~~~~~~~~~~~~~~~ and is said to build its nest on the sea in the days when there is most calm hence we derive the expression halcyon days. It was believed that the Halcyon had the power, calming the sea.

31. Design for a wallpaper or textile called 'Halcyone', 31 March, 1904 [708]
345x330
Illustrated in Durant, *Ornament . . .*, 1986
A similar design, dated June 1898, is to be found in the Print Room of the Victoria and Albert Museum

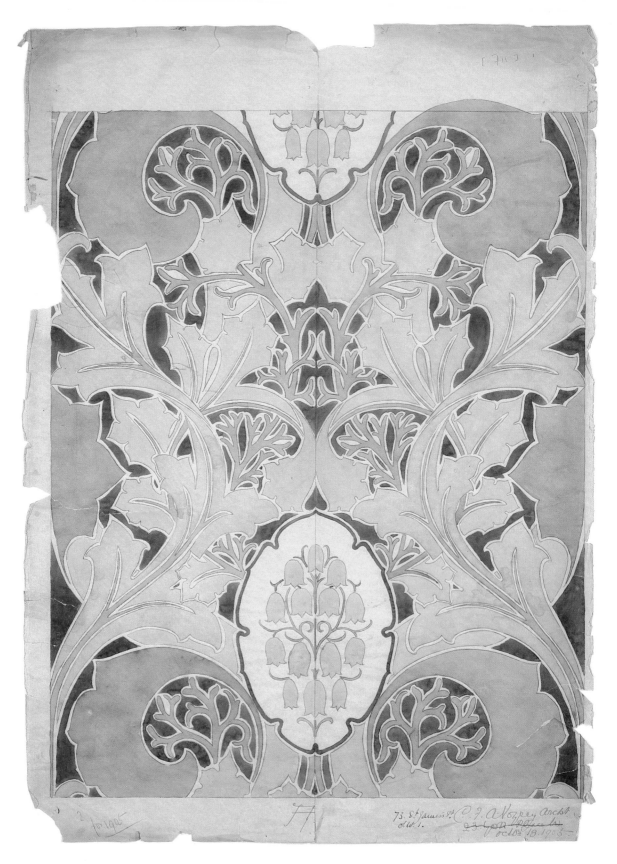

32. Design for a wallpaper, 18 October, 1905 [711]
605x315
Illustrated, *Good Furniture Magazine*, XXIII, 1924

The combination of bluebells and acanthus leaves is unusual. In general, Arts and Crafts designers preferred to base decoration entirely upon native species of plants, although the acanthus had been imported into Britain in the sixteenth and seventeenth centuries

33. Design for a wallpaper for Essex & Co,
   c. 1905 [717]
   Noted 'Essex 1905' ('1904' has been deleted)
   710x275

   The falcon - the principal motif - has been
   broken into two parts as the design was
   intended for repeat

34. Design for a wallpaper, for Essex & Co, 1906 [721]
Noted: 'For Essex 1906'
770x565

An excellent example of stylized, or 'conventional', design, a kind of design taught to students of design since the 1850s. Pugin was an early exponent - his *Floriated Ornament*, 1849, describes the method. Other designers and theorists who were expert in conventional design include: Richard Redgrave, 1808-88; J.K. Colling, 1816-1905; Christopher Dresser, 1834-1904; F.E. Hulme, 1841-1909. Gothic Revival architects often made use of conventionalized decoration

35. Design for a wallpaper, for Essex & Co, 1906 [722]
    Noted: 'Essex for 1906'
    595x570

    Like many of Voysey's decorative designs, this is deceptively simple. An examination of Morris's
    early designs will reveal, when they are compared with his mature designs, how much he had
    learned in disposing and organising the elements of a pattern. Voysey, as an architect, was particu-
    larly skilled at this

36. Design for a wallpaper, 1906 [723]
    Noted: 'Essex for 1906'
    740x550

    Voysey redrew this design in 1907, noting again 'Essex for 1906'. The reason for Voysey's duplicating of drawings is not clear; it seems probable, however, that he wished to retain a complete record of his work. His architectural *oeuvre* is among the best documented of all architects

37. Design for a wallpaper, for Sanderson & Sons, September, 1907 [727]
Noted: 'S & Sons'
750x555

By chance a curious face composed of flowers and buds appears in this design - Voysey was usually very careful to avoid such accidental occurences. Christopher Dresser, in *The Art of Decorative Design*, 1862, illustrated how such problems arose

69

38. Design for a wallpaper, for Sanderson & Sons, September, 1907 [730]
     Noted: 'S. & Sons'
     755x570

39. Design for a wallpaper, for Sanderson & Sons, 1907 [733]
    Noted: 'Sanderson & Sons, 1907'
    765x560
    The design which follows this in the RIBA Drawings Collection is dated '1916' (see Plate 40)

Voysey was reasonably busy with his architectural practice in 1907 - though not as busy as he had been in the late 1890s. Were his energies beginning to flag after a period of such intense activity? Did he have no time for decorative design? Possibly the Voysey fashion was passing

40. Design for a textile or wallpaper, 1916 [734]
Noted: 'No 126'
855x640

Voysey's architectural practice came to a virtual end with the outbreak of the 1914-1918 War. All that he actually built after this were, in fact, two war memorials - one at Malvern Wells, the other at Potter's Bar. He also remodelled a room in Harley Street and worked on architectural projects that came to nothing. During the War, Voysey wrote *Individuality* (1915), a statement of his ethical position, and began to produce decorative designs again. His skill had not left him

41. Design for a textile or wallpaper, dated December 1918 [737]
725x565
Illustrated in W.G. Paulson Townsend, *Modern Decorative Art in England*, 1922

The fluency of Voysey's brush strokes should be noted. As this design was executed on tracing-paper it is possible that he was working from a pencil outline beneath

42. A sketch for a textile design for Alexander Morton, 1918 [742]

On 17 April, 1918, Voysey wrote to Morton that he was in a 'terrible plight' financially - 'Could you give me anything to do?' Three days later Voysey wrote to Morton thanking him for his 'kind and sympathetic letter' and a cheque for £25. (See Voysey letters in the V&A Art and Design Archive)

43   Design for a wallpaper or textile called 'Peace', probably 1918 [863]
Reproduced approximately the size of the original [1″ squares]

The design commemorates the ending of the Great War

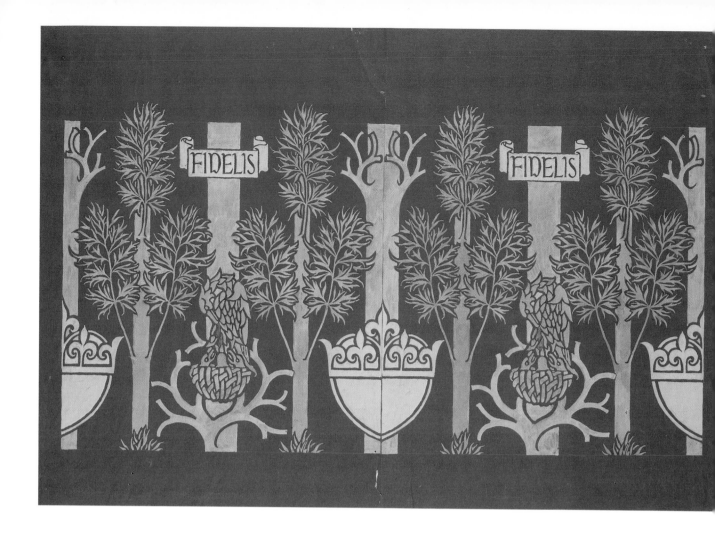

44. Design for a textile called 'Fidelis'. For Alexander Morton, December, 1919 [746]
Noted verso: 'Symbol for self-sacrifice'
375x580

The pelican feeding her young with her own blood is a traditional symbol of the sacrifice of Christ
on the Cross. (The design may possibly relate to the sacrifices made by the men and women of the
nation during the Great War.) The design is made on blueprint paper, undoubtedly because Voysey
liked its particular shade of blue. (Fidelis=Latin, 'steadfast')

45. Design for a machine-woven textile called 'Huntsman', c. 1919 [749]
585x400
Illustrated in *Good Furniture Magazine*, XXIII, 1924

This design is every bit as complex in its organization as a Morris tapestry. Nevertheless, there is a lightheartedness about it that is entirely Voysey's. It is remarkable that it was executed at a time of very considerable financial stress for Voysey. (See Plate 42)

46. Design for a textile, for Alexander Morton, c. 1920 [750]
    Noted: 'Sold to Morton for fabric, April 1920'; also: 'Drawn without cornflowers for Mrs. Hind &
    not taken'
    540x380
    Illustrated in *Good Furniture Magazine*, XXIII, 1924. A similar drawing, dated April 1920, exists
    in the Print Room of the Victoria and Albert Museum

    The sheaves of corn are symbols of plenty. The crow is a traditional symbol of hope

47. Design for a textile or wallpaper, December, 1923 [753]
   Noted: 'For sale'
   765x550

   The elements used in this design are very much the same as those that appear in Voysey's earlier designs. The colouring here, however, is typical of the early 1920s and hints, perhaps, at the influence of Claud Lovat Fraser, 1890-1921, whose brightly coloured book designs, stage sets and costumes were very popular

48. Design for a textile for the nursery, 1923 [765]
Noted 'Morton'
260x370
A similar design is to be found in the Print Room of the Victoria and Albert Museum

The image of the piper is very like that in Voysey's design for a frieze illustrated in *The Studio* in 1893

49. Design for a band of decoration called
'The Grape Stripe', 1925 [764]
Noted: 'Not sold'
570x75

Probably intended for a wallpaper

50. Design for a carpet, 1925 [766]
    Noted: 'Sold to Tomkinson March 23, 1932'
    765x570

    This would appear to be among the last decorative designs that Voysey succeeded in selling

82

51. Design for a carpet and textile, 1926 [775]
    Noted: 'Sold to Tomkinson for Carpet May 17, 1928 & Morton Sundour Fabrics'
    400x645

Bought by Speed for paper only
February 6th. 1928

C.F.A. Voysey. architect
73 St James's St. S.W.1. Feb. 19

[776] 1

52. Design for a wallpaper, February, 1928 [776]
Noted: 'Bought by Speed for paper only February 6th, 1928'
455x450

The design is based upon the eucalyptus. The design could have come from the 1890s

53. Design for a textile, called the 'Rose and Shamrock', May, 1928 [777]
765x575

The rose and shamrock together with crown probably symbolize the unity of Ireland - under the British Crown. Voysey's father, the Rev Charles Voysey, 1828-1912, was a keen supporter of the Unionist cause [The thistle, of course, refers to Scotland]

Repeat 5¼×5¼

Morton 1929

73. St James's St
S.W.1. June 1929

C.F.A.Voysey
F.R.I.B.A.
[792] 1

54. Design for a textile, June, 1929 [792]
Noted: 'Morton. 1929'
325x220

Repeat 5¼" x 4⅛"

Morton July 1929

[793]

July 1929
C.F.A.Voysey.
F.R.I.B.A.
73. St James's St SW1

55. Design for a textile, July, 1929 [793]
Noted: 'Sold to Morton, July, 1929'
280x235

A design, of Pugin-like simplicity. Executed when Voysey was in a state of considerable anxiety over his finances

56. Design for a nursery chintz called 'The House that Jack Built', September, 1929 [794]
Noted: 'Sold to Morton with all copyrights. Novr. 7 1929'
425x510

John Brandon-Jones has the following to say: 'This is an early version of a nursery chintz printed by Morton Sundour. In the final design the Rat was omitted. The figure of the "Priest" which was also omitted is a caricature of Voysey's brother who was a Unitarian minister'. (See Joanna Symonds, *C.F.A. Voysey: Catalogue of the Drawings Collection of the R.I.B.A.*, 1975)
A variant of this design was recently reproduced and sold by Habitat

Designed for printed linen. C.F. Annesley Voysey - F.R.I.B.A., R.D.I.

57. Design, probably for a nursery textile, 1929 [795]
  Noted: 'Designed for printed linen. Not taken by Morton. Copy of this, coloured, given to Maurice
  Webb for sale with copyright, June 1938.' Also: 'John Dory' [the fish]
  420x545

  It seems unlikely that Voysey would have drawn his fishes from life. They may well have been
  taken from a popular source, like Arthur Mee's *Children's Encyclopaedia*. Maurice Webb was
  probably an agent who had offered to sell Voysey's work. It is interesting to note that Voysey was
  trying to sell work in 1938 - when he was 81. This suggests that he was still worried about his
  financial position

10½ × 10½ repeat

Sold to Morton copyright in fabric only Novr. 7. 1929

[804]

58. Design for a fabric, c. 1929 [804]
Executed on tracing paper
Noted: 'Sold to Morton. Copyright in fabric only. Novr. 7 1929'
460x300

59. Design for a wallpaper, called 'Symbols of the Arts', 1930 [809]
    Noted: 'January, 1930'
    585x585

    The design was originally executed on tracing paper from which a print has been subsequently taken, thus enabling Voysey to try out various colour schemes. The palette represents painting; the mallet and chisel, carving; the dividers and proportional dividers, architecture; the lyre, music; the open book, science. The atmosphere of this design is that of the 1890s or early 1900s

91

60. Design for a wallpaper, called 'Angelic Forest', 1930 [810]
Noted: 'The Angelic Forest . . . June 1930
585x570

Voysey had painted a mural of angelic figures for Seddon to whom he was articled in 1874. It is
interesting to see him returning to the same theme some 55 years later

61. Design for a wallpaper frieze, probably intended for the nursery, 1930 [811]
Noted: 'Sold to Tomkinson Ltd'; verso: 'Copyright, for wallpaper only, is the property of
Lightbown, Aspinall & Co'
325x715

Apart from the colouring, which is like that found in children's books of the 1920s, the design
could have been made during the 1890s

62. Design, possibly for a nursery wallpaper, 1930 [812]
    Noted: 'To be hung with 12" of plain ground between each print. . . . August 1930'
    735x550

63. Design, possibly for a nursery wallpaper or a textile, called 'Great Kings and Queens', 1930 [813] 505x455

This, as the design in Plate 44, is a blue print with water-colour washes added

64. Design for a carpet, c. 1930 [846]
750x625

Like the majority of Voysey's late designs, this could have come from the 1890s. Even the
colouring is reminiscent of that era